By His Stripes We Are Healed

By
Eleanor Ment

2016

First Edition

Printed and Published by
Leiston Press
Unit 1 - 1b Masterlord Ind Estate
Leiston
Suffolk
IP16 4JD
01728 833003
www.leistonpress.com

ISBN: 978-1-911311-06-5

Dedication

To the glory of the Lord for my healing
To my family whom I love
To those who are searching: May you accept Jesus as Lord of your life and experience the peace and joy that will be yours

Contents

Preface

What happens when a young Jewish mother embraces the Christian faith which results in persecution? What does it feel like to be unemployed and then paralyzed with a back injury that leaves one bedridden and helpless?

By His Stripes We are Healed is a heart-rending story of single parenthood and the problems that were faced. It is a story of the author's miraculous healing after being bedridden and offered no hope of recovery by doctors. This true and dramatic story of perseverance and courage will touch your heart and encourage and strengthen your faith. It will bring a message of hope to those who also have a heavy cross to bear.

My Childhood

My own childhood days had been so carefree. My father was the only member of his family to survive the Nazi concentration camps – chosen to live.

His efforts were geared towards my security and happiness. We lived in a middle class home in Bulawayo Zimbabwe, where my parents had a bakery business. Worn by toil, they left early each morning at 5 am and would return late at night. I will never forget that haven of safety - swinging in the little garden which was adorned with fruit trees. There was a fire place near the backdoor which led to the kitchen. We used to heat up the water when any of us wanted a bath.

Our home was one of real Orthodox Jews. Fastened in a slanting position on the right hand post of the front door was a Mezuzah. Most Jewish homes have at least one of these. It consists of a piece of parchment made up of skin of a clean animal, on which is written Deut. 6: 4-9and 11:18-21, rolled into a little scroll and enclosed in a metal, wooden or plastic tube. Whenever we left or entered the house my parents and myself would touch the Mezuzah and then kiss the hand that had done so.

I had a wide circle of Jewish friends at junior school, yet my best friend Dee was a Gentile, the only Gentile friend I had. She was a willowy girl with a short mop of platinum blond hair cascading down past her shoulders and light blue eyes. I would frequently spend weekends at her home, but I was only allowed to go after we had celebrated the Sabbath on Friday evenings. Then we would attend the evening service at the synagogue.

Afterwards at home we shared the traditional Jewish dinner. My father would pour the grape juice into a glass and bless the food: ‘ This is a symbol of joy and gladness, hence its sweetness.’ Having drunk of this cup my father would bless the two loaves of bread which were a reminder of God’s faithfulness to his people by providing manna in the wilderness, and a double portion for the Sabbath (Exodus 16: 13-30).

In this manner we would remember the Sabbath, thus following the commandment given to Moses on Mount Sinai. And as I watched my father’s hands break the bread I knew that he would remember his own past deprivations and suffering. I would not be allowed to do anything on the Sabbath for it is the day of rest, not even read or sew. I observed all the traditions of a typical Orthodox Jew, but all the time I had a questioning in my soul that asked why we did these things. Why was I different from my friend Dee? She did not go to church on Friday night and she seemed happy. We were different or was she different? When I visited Dee I always found it strange that her family did not observe any religious customs at all, not even grace before meals.

At school it was compulsory for all scholars to attend religious instructions, so we were grouped according to our religion. As a Jew I was taught by a Rabbi. I recall listening attentively one day as the Rabbi told us that we as Jews were still awaiting our Messiah. I pondered each word as he spoke; But Jehovah has given to His people the wonderful promise that in His time He will send His anointed One, the Messiah, who shall free Israel from all her oppressors.'

On returning home one day I told my mother of the Rabbi's words....

'Quite right,' mom replied, 'So we, as Jews, do not believe in Jesus,' I was left to wonder with anticipation about when our Messiah would eventually arrive.

Besides the Sabbath our family celebrated all the Jewish festivals and feasts. I once asked the Rabbi why God had appointed so many feasts for Israel - ' Because he wanted his people to be a joyous people, 'he replied. And indeed our family was a joyous one.

In April we celebrated the Passover, or Pesach, as we called it. This was to commemorate the passing of the Lord over those Israelites homes of which the lintels and door posts were sprinkled with the blood of the lamb. It was to commemorate their deliverance from bondage in Egypt. It was also known as the Feast of Unleavened Bread, so during the eight days I was forbidden to eat bread, but ate Matzoth instead. At Pesach dinner there were always bitter herbs for us to eat in memory of the bitter times our forefathers endured in Egypt. And my mother would always place a shank bone of lamb on the table to remind us of the blood that was sprinkled on the doors of the chosen ones.

As a child I never questioned the multitude of customs and feasts we observed throughout the year. There was Purim which takes place in March, a day of festivity, rejoicing and the giving of presents to celebrate the deliverance of Israel in the time of Queen Esther. There was the more serious and inspiring day of Rosh Ha-Shana or New Year in September. In the synagogue a Shofar which is a ram's horn is blown as a reminder of the ram Abraham sacrificed in place of Isaac. The shofar is curved, a symbol that man must bend his will before God. Then ten days thereafter was Yom Kippur, the Day of Atonement. This marked the day when the Israelites repented for worshiping the golden calf. On this day many Jews stand in the synagogue fasting for twenty five hours, abstaining even from water. Five days later we celebrated the Succoth or Feast of Tabernacles marking a change from solemnity to joy. For this feast signified the gratitude of Israel for God's providence during their years of wandering in the wilderness.

Such customs of gratitude and celebration were close to home for my family.

Indeed, such customs were a mark of unity and warmth in our home. There was such a strong bond of unity and security that I never imagined a life without it.

The scars of deprivation my father bore from his days in the concentration camp remained even during the happy days. He would always insisted that no food ever be left wasted at our table. He would often shut himself in his bedroom for hours in deep depression and no one was allowed to disturb him while he lay in bed oblivious of anyone else outside the closed doors of his room.

LEAVING HOME

During my youth and teenage years my social circle was just as sheltered and secure as was my family's home. On weekends I would attend Jewish youth movement meetings in a large hall in town. We would participate in debates and seminars, and sometimes we went away together on youth camps. Often the revisionist group I had joined held a summer camp in Port Elizabeth. We worked well together as a group, sharing the chores and the fun. Much of the time en route and at the camp fire was spent gaily singing Hebrew songs.

After one of these camps in December I took a train to Cape Town to spend the rest of my vacation with an aunt and uncle. They owned a beautiful two storey house, and I shared a room with my mother who had also joined us from Bulawayo. I fell in love with the beauty of Cape Town with it's surrounding mountains and it's vast beaches of pure white sand. Standing on Signal Hill taking in the breath taking view of the whole lit up city, I somehow knew that I would be returning to live there one day. Little did I know then of the trying circumstances I would later encounter there.

Back in Bulawayo I attended a high school quite a distance from home in an isolated bushy area. Each day I would ride for half an hour on my bicycle to school. School would commence each day with an assembly which the Jewish scholars were not compelled to attend. Yet somehow I felt drawn to the place and would be the only Jewish scholar present. Hymns were sung and verses of scripture read. It was here that the Word of God started opening up to me. The verses of scripture from the New Testament seemed so real and alive. The meaning of each word and phrase was immediately apparent to me. Each day we would sing the Lord's prayer, and I would wonder why we Jews could not believe in Jesus when His teachings were so beautiful And how could the Jews reject someone who not only did good, but performed so many miracles. My faith grew like an underground stream, quite hidden but strong. Was this Jesus not our long-awaited Messiah?

The headmaster accepted my presence with equanimity as only gentile scholars attended assembly due to scriptures being read out from the New Testament. It was not long before a Jewish scholar approached me and asked me why I was attending assembly. I replied that I felt a compulsion I could not fully understand. My explanation was received with an expression of perplexity mixed with rebuke. Deep inside of me I knew there had always been an unfulfilled feeling as though my soul was searching for something. It could not be friends, for I had friends. It could not be love, for my parents loved me. What was this something that gnawed at my very soul?

By the time I was in Standard 10 the political upheaval in Zimbabwe had reached a climax. Because our school was so isolated, the army was called in for our protection. All the huge tanks and machine guns at the entrance gate and the guards in khaki uniforms contributed to a general sense of unease within me. I wanted space and peace, and this is what Cape Town stood for in my imagination. I would often daydream about the Cape, and picture the waves rushing up against the rocks, the white stretch of beach and the exhilarating sensation of the salty wind against my face. I longed to live by the seaside and watch the waves crashing against the rocks and run on the white sand of the beach.

Soon my father and I were to discuss my future. My father was a brilliant intellectual man. Trained as an interpreter, he could fluently read and write seven different languages. Yet he found that he could not make a sufficient living with his degree, so after long hours at the bakery, he would work late into the night translating for various companies for extra money. He was a man who inspired much respect, yet he was a humble man and satisfied with few material possessions. His main concerns were to provide a home, food and security for himself and his family.

My father was very insistent that I learn something useful when I left school, something which could be used all over the world to support myself.

'Attend college for a year and do a private secretarial course,' he advised me. I watched his face to see if he were going to say more, and then he added. 'I am sure you will be married one day and have children and then what would you do with a degree?' I knew he would add these words. My parents were keen for me to find a husband. For them, the protection of a husband signified the future they desired for me. I knew that mom would not rest till I was happily married. She hoped for me to be safely wed by the age of 21. She did not want me to be on my own out there in the world.

Working in an office as a secretary never really interested me. I was more inclined towards something in the medical field like physiotherapy. I received sufficient grades at school to pursue an academic career. Still I thought carefully about my father's advice. I felt it was only fair to listen to him. What if he did spend a fortune on a degree for me and in the end I wasted it?'

'Okay, dad, you win,' I replied.

Deep down, however, I was disappointed that I could not pursue the career I wanted to. Soon I was asking my parents if I could take up my career in Cape Town. Though my parents were not at all keen for me to live on my own in a strange city, they let me go on condition I stayed with my aunt and uncle and attend college. On the last day of school I felt a lump in my throat as our headmaster shook my hand. 'May the Lord be with you,' he said in a gently affirmative tone. I swung around on hearing these words and smiled a final goodbye. No one had ever said that to me before.

Weeks later I was on the train as it chugged away from Bulawayo station. I waved goodbye to my parents who were very heart sore to see me leave home. I felt as though the train were conveying me over the threshold of adulthood.

Would I find the something I had been searching for?

Would this yearning in my soul come to rest once I had left my familiar world?' Time alone would tell. Yet I felt an excitement in my spirit at a whole new world in another country with a different environment and people that I was yet to meet. New horizons were opening up for me!

LIGHT AND DARKNESS

Be not unequally yoked together with unbelievers; for what fellowship hath righteousness with unrighteousness? And what communion has light with darkness? 2 Cor:6:14

I was warmly welcomed in Cape Town and in no time I was settled into my aunt and uncle's glorious double storey house. I soon adjusted to the new routine and different environment.

I loved the sea and feeling the waves splashing against my feet while I walked on the sand. I had missed the sea, while living in Bulawayo, and I spent weekends at the beautiful beaches in Cape Town enjoying the sunshine and swimming with the waves coming up towards me. I was just 18 years old and swimming quite far out when a 'backwash' of sea water went over my head. I went under water a few times with the torrent of water crashing over me and thought I was going to drown. I cried out to God to help me and a miracle happened with the next huge wave I was washed to shore and managed to run onto the sand. I thanked God for His Hand on my life and that He had spared me. I was quite shaken by the experience of nearly drowning and sat on the beach with a towel wrapped around me watching people swimming for the rest of the afternoon. I would be very careful from now on not to swim too far out. I had failed to see a notice nearby warning swimmers of the 'backwash'. My thoughts raced, how quickly one could be ushered into eternity. There must be a purpose for my life.

The college I attended was half an hour's walk from home and I had soon made many friends. I enjoyed my studies at College and the lovely walk there. After initially living with my aunt and uncle I moved to a boarding house run by Catholic nuns. I stayed at the boarding house for the rest of the time I was studying at College. The boarding house was peaceful to reside at and I watched the nuns serving us meals daily and praying. The days seemed to fly by till the next thing I knew I had received my secretarial certificate. No sooner had this happened when I received a surprise call from my parents.

'El, we have decided to follow suit and move to Cape Town!' exclaimed my mother.' 'Yes, it's true,' said my dad. 'We are leaving Bulawayo to join you. I was thrilled with their decision, as were my uncle and aunt.

My cousin, Ruth, was expecting her first child, and she and her husband had decided to buy a house. They arranged for my parents to take over the lease of their lovely apartment which was situated by the sea.

I resumed attendance of the services at the Sea Point synagogue with parents on Friday evenings. I recall listening attentively one evening to the Rabbi as he said:

'Hear, O Israel, the Lord our God is one Lord, the Shema, the cornerstone of our faith, the watchword of the Jewish people. Our God is One.'

At this stage I began to experience an inner conflict as I wrestled with the opposing doctrines of the exclusiveness of the Jewish definition of God and the Christian beliefs I had been influenced by at school. I was not one to go with the crowd simply because I was born into a particular culture. My sense of commitment and conviction in what I believed had always been strong. But I was now confused at the Christian belief in three Gods. And there was no one I knew that could explain this to me either. Deep inside of me I wrestled with so many questions, why were we born, why did we have to die, what was the purposes of life and why was there so much suffering? I was sure that one day God would reveal Himself to me and then all the questions I had would be settled in my mind.

Nevertheless, I continued to enjoy a wide circle of Jewish friends.

One evening when we were all going out together in a crowd I was introduced to an attractive Jewish man.

'Eleanor,' said my friend, 'I have someone I'd like you to meet.'

I looked at the well-built man in front of me and held out my hand in greeting. I smiled as he shook my hand.

'Eleanor, this is Abe ((not his real name).

'Hello,' I said, warmly, taking to Abe immediately.

Abe and I went out for a few dates, then, for a long while I did not hear from him. I was so disappointed and began to date other men but somehow I really wanted to see this man who seemed so right for me. Praying at night in my bedroom, I asked God to let me see him again. Miraculously God answered my prayers. Abe phoned me. That was the first time I'd really gone on my knees and prayed earnestly for something. I had prayed in synagogues before, but not at such length and with such intensity. It was seven months since I had seen Abe.

Soon we were going out on a steady basis. Many things attracted me to him. He was of average height and well-built with dark brown eyes. He was a good conversationalist and a charming companion. He had a keen sense of humour and enjoyed sport, like myself. We would often go and watch soccer matches together over weekends. His brothers and sisters were all married with children, and my heart warmed to the way Abe used to play with them. He will make a good father, I thought.

My parents were fond of Abe, and when he proposed to me they were thrilled, not least of all because he was an Orthodox Jew. My mother, I think, was almost more excited that I was. She could not wait for me to experience the same extreme happiness she had found in her marriage with my father. In her mind, marriage meant all the things dad had given her, love, affection, companionship, understanding and security.

Soon all the preparations were made for our wedding. Then something happened that made me doubt my future with Abe. In writing the list of 500 guests I had inadvertently omitted to add one of Abe's nephews to the list. When he discovered this he flew into a range which I was quite unprepared for

This incident gave rise to apprehension within me which began to grow day by day. My mother was present on the afternoon when I promptly gave Abe his ring back. My mother quietened Abe and with her soothing tongue she reconciled us. 'Come on you two,' she said, ' all the preparations have been made. You cannot let a small argument create a rift now.' Yet I felt uneasy about going into this marriage having witnessed Abe's temper.

It was of immense importance to my mother that I did not ruin this opportunity for marriage. Had I taken my own reservations about Abe seriously I would have resisted and been patient till I had met someone more suitable. As it was, most of my friends were either married or on the brink of doing so even though they were in their early twenties. Partnerships develop very quickly in a closely-knit community such as ours was. In the end, I trusted my mother's optimism and succumbed to her pleas.

On my wedding day the weather was gloriously warm and I was excited about the prospect of being married, but even then, I had a sense of foreboding that was hard to shake off.

Most of the 500 people invited to our wedding attended both the synagogue and the reception. The only dark cloud that day was one guest's private words to me. She said that she did not feel we were suited for one another. However, I refused to let her words undermine the joy I was experiencing. Basically I still believed that I had finally married the man I wanted.

Considering the fact that I was only 21, my expectations of marriage were not idealistically high. I wanted mutual love and companionship, someone with whom I could share my hopes and aspirations. I wanted a man who would be a good father to our children and provide a secure home, with my help and support.

Two are better than one because they have a good return for their work. If one falls down his friend can help him up. But pity the man who falls and has no one to help him up   Ecclesiastes4:9

But from the beginning the reality was different to the dream. Abe did not provide the warmth and affection that I was used to in my own family. Within weeks I felt I could not endure this marriage with all the abuse. I told my mother that I wanted to leave Abe and she was horrified. She did not want her dreams for me to be shattered; she failed to realize that they were already ruined. She tried to convince me it was just a phase that would pass.

So I persevered and proceeded to raise a family. I thought that our three children might help mend the rift, hoping all the time that things would improve. But they did not.

I hardly had enough money for essentials so my parents would give me a bit of pocket money in order to buy some clothes for the children. As soon as the children were a little older I took them to a crèche and went out to work. The inevitable break came when the crèche phoned to say that Jeremy, our eldest son was getting sick every day and they suspected it was a result of turmoil at home. This was the final straw. I filed for divorce. I felt compelled to bring this intolerable union to an end. It was not an easy decision to make. I was aware of the disastrous effects it could have on everyone involved. It was a devastating experience, but after agonizingly weighing up all of the circumstances and my own ability to cope I left my husband and moved out with my children.

At a later stage in my life the Lord showed me how He had to separate **light** from **darkness**.

Our three children were still very young when our marriage ended. Our marriage lasted exactly seven years. After the divorce Abe would see the children on weekends but he seldom took them for the holidays. There was no granny or grandpa on his side to fuss over them.

While we were married Abe had remarked that I wasn't very 'Jewish'. This was because I did not keep up with all the Jewish traditions, some of which I felt no longer applied. For this reason he inserted a clause in our divorce papers which stated categorically that our three children were to be brought up in the Jewish faith and to have a Hebrew education. This very clause was eventually used to the Lord's glory and to relieve me of one of many future burdens.

After my divorce we moved in temporarily with two of my friends, Carl and Sue, My parents were getting on in years and they lived in a very small apartment. They could not afford to accommodate me and three rowdy children. But they helped whenever they could and sometimes gave me money to buy groceries for the children. Room was made in Carl and Sue's attic for the children and I was given the guest room. The children adjusted to the upheaval and were soon enjoying the lovely garden and swimming pool. I was taking the divorce hard and wanted nothing more than to be left alone in my room reading.

After three months of Carl and Sue's loyal support and encouragement I was feeling much better. I eventually heard of a reasonable rental apartment near the children's school and within walking distance from town. From outside the apartment seemed in fair condition, but once inside I saw how dilapidated it was. At least it would be a roof over our heads.

Soon we had moved in and I was busy unpacking. When the children returned from school the place looked quite liveable. But on closer inspection I was in for a shock. It had begun to rain, and the more it rained the more the water began to seep in until there was a persistent, discordant dripping through the lounge roof. Checking the electrical plugs I discovered that the kitchen was infested with cockroaches. There ugly creatures kept coming up from the drains and peering at me. The kitchen floors were rotting away and tiles were missing on the walls. I asked myself aloud, 'What can I expect for such a cheap rental?' I felt as if I could tolerate anything rather than a disastrous marriage but I was disappointed that I could not provide a more comfortable home for my young children.

I spent the weekend cleaning and painting while the children played in the park opposite us. I took a moment off and watched them playing happily, with not a care in the world.

There was Jeremy with his thick mop of dark hair, catching the ball that Mervyn had thrown him. And Mervyn had dark blonde hair looking so cute and cuddly. Amy, the youngest was much smaller with light brown hair and hazel eyes. She looked every bit of a little girl with her hair cropped to her shoulders in cascading curls. I remembered the day after she had her hair cut, when I had just fetched her from the crèche, with Mervyn sitting in the car alongside her.

'Did they like your hair at the crèche, Amy?' Mervyn asked

Amy shrugged her shoulders and replied, 'I supposed so'

At home it dawned on me how hard it was being a single parent trying to raise three boisterous young children, and at the same time handling a full-time job. I felt I owed my children so much to compensate them, yet there was so little money to accomplish this. The amount of maintenance Abe paid each month was negligible compared to what we needed. It hardly covered the bare necessities. I had come for a relatively comfortable home. The adjustment necessary was considerable. Furthermore, it was difficult to see my children in less fortunate surrounding and being denied the luxuries which their playmates enjoyed. I could not afford to give them as many treats as I wished to. These things penetrated deep into my heart. I wanted my children to feel secure in their environment and to have a happy childhood. I wanted the very best for them but I had hold on and trust that there would be better times ahead for us.

FROM JUDAISM TO CHRISTIANITY

- PERSECUTION

When thou passest through the water, I will be with thee, and through the rivers, they shall not overflow thee; when though walkest through the fire, thou shall not be burned, neither shall the flame kindle upon thee. *Isaiah 43:2*

With all the added responsibilities of single parenthood I started yielding to anxiety. Much of my time was spent worrying. Would I be able to fulfil my children's needs on my own? I joined a support group which was a great help and encouragement. It was there that I met Toni. She lectured at the club and there was something different about her, something unusual, almost unique. A thought surfaced in my mind. Did she not have that same expression of absolute peace on her face that I had noticed in my headmaster all those years back? After the lecture was over I approached her and asked her how she found such peace with all the turmoil about us. "It's Jesus," she replied, and then she queried, "Are you a believer at all?" "Well I guess I am in a way." I found myself saying. This was because when I heard the scriptures read out from the New Testament in Assembly at school in Bulawayo I believed in the Lord Jesus Christ. Then she asked me if I would like to pray a prayer of commitment with her. I phoned her the following day and we spontaneously began to pray together over the telephone. *"Dear Lord Jesus, I need you, have mercy on me and forgive me my sins. Thank you for dying on the cross for my sins. Thank you that you are alive. I want to ask you to take over my life as my Lord and Saviour. Thank you for giving your followers eternal life. Help me to follow you daily."* As I accepted Jesus as my personal Saviour I felt a beautiful wave of peace come over me. After that Toni and I began to pray together regularly. Toni would invite me to her home frequently. I remember one such afternoon in her comfortable lounge when she spoke to me of her commitment and of how she became a believer. She served muffins and Ceylon tea that day. The more I listened to her the more I began to accept Jesus as my personal Saviour with a newer, stronger conviction than ever before. Soon a newfound joy began to flood my entire being and I had inner peace. I wanted to tell everyone how I felt, and I did. Since high school I had accepted Jesus instinctively but secretly. My love for Him had been subsequently suppressed especially during my marriage to an Orthodox Jew who felt that I was not 'Jewish enough.' Now I felt free to express my Christian love without restraint, with outspoken enthusiasm. When I began to confess my faith to people I was quite taken aback at the reaction of people who had long been friends of mine, many of whom rejected me because of my new found faith. Toni, the lecturer who had led me to the Lord, was by now a firm friend and she provided immense support. She invited me to attend church with her and she made an appointment for me to see her Pastor. I was told why it was important for us as believers to go through the waters of baptism. I was soon baptised in obedience to the Lord Jesus Christ. I felt like an angel dressed in a white cloak with my shoulder length hair cascading down. I felt sad that none of my family were with me to witness this wonderful occasion. The congregation watched as I went into the water and faced the Pastor, Rex Morris

"Eleanor, do you believe Jesus is the Son of God, do you believe He died for your sins?" he asked.

"Yes," I replied.

"Well then nothing hinders you from being baptised; I now baptise you in the name of the Father, the Son and the Holy Spirit."

I felt myself going under water completely and then rising up again. There was such fulfilment and gratitude as he blessed me with those words. Afterwards Toni invited me and some of the congregation to her home to enjoy a lovely spread of eats in celebration. I was overwhelmed with gratitude and a new peace began to flood my entire being. I began to take Jeremy with me to bible study, as he was old enough to understand, and I took the younger children to church each Sunday morning. One evening after bible study, while ascending the staircase I heard voices in our apartment. I wondered who could be visiting so late and was aghast to open the door and find Abe glaring angrily at me. I immediately asked Jeremy to go to bed. "How dare you take the children inside a church," he shouted, shaking his fist at me. "You know the clause we agreed to. These children are Jewish and I forbid them to be taken to church. When they are older they can choose, but right now they are to be brought up in the Jewish faith." I tried to explain to Abe that I was still a Jew even though I believed Jesus was our Messiah, but he was too angry to listen. I heaved a sigh of relief when he left slamming the door behind him.

I tiptoed into Jeremy's room. He was lying wide awake and must have heard all the commotion. I sat next to his bed and told him that the Lord was in control of everything, so he must get some sleep and then I kissed him goodnight. I found it hard to sleep myself. All the shouting had brought to mind the terrible memories of my stormy marriage. I questioned the children the next day. Apparently Abe had telephoned to speak to the children and Amy had told him I was at church with Jeremy. From then on I literally had to smuggle my children to church. And when I decided to have them dedicated to the Lord I could not take them inside the church; they had to be dedicated in the apartment, but they were dedicated nevertheless! After this incident, I felt I should speak to my parents about my conversion before they heard it from anyone else. I telephoned first.

Dad answered: "Hello El," he said.

"Hello Dad, may I come and see you and Mom? I have something to tell you."

There was a nervous edge to my voice.

"Sure, is everything okay?" he asked.

"I'm fine Dad, I'll be there just now." "Something must be up," Dad said. "You never phone first; you just pop in."

"Dad I'll speak to you in a few minutes," I said, and hung up. It was about a fifteen minute drive to my parents' apartment. I prayed all the way in the car. As I ascended the staircase my heart began to pound. "Here goes," I thought. I was not looking forward to this task.

"Well," Dad said, "it sounded as if you had something urgent that you had to tell us." I slowly sat on the couch and took a deep breath.

"Mom, Dad, I love you both so much," I quavered, "and I really appreciate the wonderful parents you've been to me." I swallowed, and took another deep breath, and then I just blurted out: "I've become a believer!"

Mom and Dad both looked stunned by the news. There was a long moment of silence. "Does that mean . . ." Dad began to ask.

"It means that I believe in God, I believe that the bible is the Word of God and I believe that Jesus is the Messiah."

If I dropped a bomb it would not have been received with more shock. At first they were speechless and all I could hear was my heart throbbing wildly. The expression on my mother's face seemed to say, "After all we have done for you this is how you repay us." Dad put his arm around her to try and comfort her. Her expression had turned to one of utter dismay and astonishment. More moments of dead silence followed, then my mother said: "This is the worst thing you could ever have done to us."

In a way I could understand. They felt as if they had been betrayed by their own flesh and blood. Yet their response cast such a shadow on my happiness since my conversion.

"Mom, I still love you and Dad. Nothing has changed my love for you. I am just a believer," I said. I sighed.

This was about the hardest thing I had ever had to do. They had so carefully brought me up in the Jewish faith, faithfully observing each and every festival and custom; always explaining everything to me in detail and here I was believing what I had been told not to. The situation became more awkward. Neither of us had anything to say. I squirmed uncomfortably and finally decided to leave them and give them a chance to sort out their own feelings. They had had enough of a shock and I enough stress. But I was soon to face more. News of my conversion spread like wildfire throughout the Jewish community. One evening there was a knock at the door. It was the Cantor of the synagogue I used to attend. I was surprised and could see the fury in his eyes but I greeted him politely, having decided not to alienate anyone because of my Christianity, no matter how they insulted me.

"Well, young lady, I've heard of your conversion," he said abruptly. "I can't believe that you have gone against everything you were brought up with." His voice became louder as he spoke. " I don't care how much water has been poured over your head, you are still Jewish!" He was shaking his arm and pointing his finger at me while he spoke. His gestures were so exaggerated as to be comic. I almost wanted to laugh. Then I became more serious.

"I know I'm Jewish," I replied, "I'm a completed Jew. Jesus was a Jew. He said that his people hated Him without a cause. He is our Messiah."

"Enough of that!" the Cantor shouted and suddenly left, slamming the door behind him. I was becoming quite accustomed to slammed doors, yet each time it hurt afresh, especially the fact that no one was prepared to try and understand that it was no contradiction to be a Jewish believer. Shortly after that episode, I received a call from the secretary of the Hebrew school my children were attending asking me to come in and see the principal. Feeling a bit apprehensive I entered his office. He looked me straight in the eye and came right to the point: "Mrs Ment, it has come to our notice that you have accepted the Christian faith. In a case like this one, where the mother adopts a faith other than the Jewish one, we feel it is in the best interests of the children to remove then from the Hebrew school. As you know, we adhere strictly to Jewish traditions and Judaism."

I sighed! It was only the middle of the academic year and it would be difficult to get them into another school. I pleaded with him to keep the children on till the end of the year, but he was adamant. And I was right. It was more than difficult. I tried just about every school in the Cape Peninsula but all were booked up till January. My Pastor called a special meeting to pray about this issue. A group of believers knelt down with me to pray for my children. I was not alone; my brothers and sisters in the Lord were with me in my crisis. "Eleanor's suffering is our suffering," the Pastor said. I shall never forget those words.

Then one of the members came up to me with a suggestion. "Eleanor, why don't you show the Hebrew school your consent papers which state that the children have to have a Hebrew education and have to be brought up in the Jewish faith."

What a wise answer the Lord had given him! I followed his suggestion and soon afterwards received a letter saying that my children could not only stay at the Hebrew school, but, because of my circumstances they would educate them at no cost to me whatsoever. This was nothing short of a miracle and I can remember going down on my knees and praising God. What the enemy meant for evil the Lord turned around for good.

I knew those determined to follow Christ at any cost may well expect to face opposition or ridicule from family and friends.

Sometime after my conversion I was invited to a Bar Mitzvah service. At the age of thirteen each Jewish boy is made a 'Son of the Commandment' (Bar Mitzvah) and after this he is held responsible for his own sins. The Bar Mitzvah service includes the calling up of the boy to read a passage from the Law and he may also give a suitable address during the festivities that follow. Abe had insisted that both our sons have a Bar Mitzvah. At the time I had questioned my Christian friends as to what I should do. We all decided that Jesus had a Bar Mitzvah and, if our Lord could do so, there was no harm in my sons doing the same. It was the first time I had been inside a synagogue since my conversion. In the orthodox synagogue the women all sit in the upper gallery. I watched the service from above, seeing the Rabbi seated away from everyone else, and the men and young boys with their talliths (praying shawls) wrapped around their shoulders and yamikas (skull caps) worn on their heads. All the ladies were beautifully dressed and most of them wore hats to match their outfits. The huge chandeliers above lit up the whole synagogue with its beautiful wine coloured carpets and stained glass windows. I looked at all these Jewish people and prayed silently for them to come to know their Messiah. A Jewish lady whom I had never seen before had come to sit beside me. She soon began to chat to me. Suddenly she leaned over me and whispered:

"You know, I am a clairvoyant."

'Oh my goodness so many people were in deception and searching for truth,' I thought. I prayed quietly to the Lord for protection.

With a gasp I whispered back. "In the Old Testament in Deuteronomy and in Isaiah God denounces anything to do with spiritualism." Then I quoted from Isaiah 8:10:

"When men tell you to consult mediums and spiritists who whisper and mutter, should not people enquire of their God? Why consult the dead on behalf of the living?" Isaiah 8:19 NIV

The lady argued with me and said that she enjoyed what she was doing and that it gave her peace.

"That peace is not of God," I replied.

It seemed amazing that out of all the people in the entire synagogue and all the empty chairs she had come to sit beside me. I felt that the Lord had placed her next to me to warn her. I explained that I stood for God and I challenged her to search the scriptures. But I left the service with a heavy heart. Here was this lady who was accepted amongst the Jewish community yet she was involved in spiritualism which God abhors. And here I was, ostracized by the Jewish community because I had accepted Jesus as my Messiah. How many Jewish people do not even know the contents of the Old Testament properly. Nor did I before my conversion. Yet there are so many Old Testament prophecies pointing to our Messiah. Oh how I pray that my people will search the scriptures. I long to see more of them come to know the Lord. "Well," I thought, "the Lord has not finished with the Jewish people." His word says:

"*Israel has experienced a hardening in part until the full number of the Gentiles has come in.*" *Romans 11:25 NIV*

I made up my mind to intercede for my people and pray for the peace of Jerusalem (see Psalm 122:6). Little did I know that the Lord was not finished with me either. I was yet to be humbled through a series of circumstances before I would be graced with my own special way of spreading His Word.

LIFE GOES ON

Nine years had passed since my divorce. Jeremy was 16, Mervyn 13 and Amy 12 years of age. I was still attending church on a regular basis. One Sunday instead of attending my own church I decided to attend a service at another church. As the pews were being occupied with people I glanced around. With few exceptions the whole congregation consisted of couples with their children. I again experienced an inexplicable emptiness inside me as I watched families sitting together. I longed for Jeremy, Mervyn and Amy to be with me. Everyone seemed so content and they just took it for granted that their families were in the Lord's house with them. However it was going to be a spiritual battle before this would happen in my life. It was becoming increasingly difficult to take my children to church and I invariably went on my own. It was while I was in church that I met an elderly couple, Ethnie and Len.

As I sat next to them in the pew they introduced themselves and I proudly said. "I am a Jewish believer."

They took to me immediately as they loved the Jewish people. The elderly lady was to become my spiritual mother. She was a woman strong in faith, and often we would pray together on the telephone, or we would get together for a time of prayer. Every day she prayed faithfully for me and the children. The Lord had sent this beautiful person to brighten my life! I was working in an industrial area far out of town and the travelling was tiresome. I decided to seek another job. Ethnie and Len began to pray that I find work in town. It was an employer's market and jobs were scarce in Cape Town at that time. I applied for two jobs and to my surprise I was offered both. One was in the private sector with beautiful office accommodation. This job required me to start immediately. The other was in a Government department and required me to start a month later. Both positions were in town and both offered the same salary. After much deliberation I eventually chose the job in the private sector.

One always has to be on one's guard against the enemy's traps Sometimes things look like a rose but it is not a rose once you move into the situation.

This job seemed so attractive from outward appearances but little did I realize the immense pressure it would involve and the stress that I would endure as a result of my decision. As soon as I had commenced my duties I realized how hectic it was and how my employers would exploit my services. I had four bosses who were all demanding, each urgently wanting his work done immediately. In spite of my assistant's help I was exhausted at the end of each day. In the evenings the children were equally demanding of my attention. I had to cook dinner, wash clothes, supervise their homework and spend time with them generally. On weekends I would be busy catching up with housework. There was scarcely any time to rest or socialize. Yet as one pressure or problem dissolved another would replace it. Work became more and more hectic and I would usually have to work overtime to keep up. The children were getting older and were developing new needs. I began to feel concerned that I was hardly available for heart to heart communication with them and they were at the ages when they needed it the most.

Nevertheless, because of all the pressure at my job it prompted me to look for another job. I was soon offered a job in the personnel section of a large company just up the road. I promptly typed out my resignation and handed it in. One of my bosses tried to persuade me that I was making a mistake: "Eleanor," he said kindly, "you're moving from the frying pan into the fire. Believe me. I worked for that company. Many people, including myself were out of work through them. Withdraw your resignation." Still I took no heed of his warning. I decided I wanted to leave. I felt that work could not be more pressurised than the company I was working at and I need a change. And I was about to find out that this would get progressively worse!

PART 2

REPERCUSSIONS

I have never felt such a deep emptiness in mind and in soul as I felt when driving home from work that afternoon. Every seemed like a bad dream. It was as if I had lost my own identity; as if I were being carried away by some uncontrollable current.

I thought about Mervyn. Mervyn had excelled at sport and had won the Victor Ludorum at school for athletics. There were cups and certificates on our wall unit showing his achievements. He was achieving in the things he enjoyed and I was proud of him.

It was towards the end of that year when an acquaintance introduced me to a man a little older than myself. I looked at this slender built man with light brown curly hair and deep blue eyes and took to him immediately. He was well dressed and groomed and did not look old enough to be a father of teenage daughters. He was softly spoken and loved the Lord. His wife had left him and married someone else before he came to know the Lord and his two teenage daughters were staying with him. We attended church services together and he would fetch and take me to our prayer meetings and bible studies. Ivan (not his real name) was a Jewish believer like myself. It was good to have a friend in my life who believed like I did.

One evening we attended a church service and left the service feeling really blessed. It was bitterly cold and as I prepared to enter the car, I momentarily placed my bible on the boot of Ivan's car so that I could put my jacket on. Forgetting the bible we drove off. Prior to the service, Ivan had bought some fruit and vegetables and placed them on the back seat of the car. Suddenly he took a sharp turn and the fruit and vegetables were strewn all over the seat. He had driven quite a long way at a moderate speed when a verse of scripture flashed through my mind. It was then that I remembered that I had placed my bible on the outside boot of the car! I asked Ivan to stop. Ivan immediately pulled the car over to the side of the road and I jumped out. There was my bible in exactly the same position that I had placed it – it had not moved! How great is the Lord His angel must have had his hand on my bible making sure it did not fall off on the outside boot of Ivan's car. The Lord was reminding me of His power and strength.

My parents became quite fond of Ivan. By then they had almost accepted the fact that I was a believer although Mom still couldn't get used to the idea that I was going to church instead of synagogues. At least there was a breakthrough now from all the prayers for my father and mother. My heart went out to them and

I longed for them to come to know their Messiah. But I left them in the hands of the Lord.

No man can come to me, except the Father which hath sent me draw him: and I will raise him up in the last day. .John 6:44

BACK TROUBLE

My grace is sufficient for thee; for my strength is made perfect in weakness. 2 Cor. 12:9

In the interim, the time had come for me to commence my duties at my new Job. I left home early for work that day. It was a beautiful morning. I took in a few deep breaths of fresh air and felt confident that things were going to improve. I had made sure I went to bed early for a few nights and this restored my energy. I felt sure that things would improve with the new job and increased salary.

However, any pressure that I had been under at the previous company was nothing compared to what I was now about to experience. I was appointed to the Personnel Section which was in utter chaos. Telephones were ringing incessantly, letters of appointment had to be typed, interviews organized and people had to be screened by telephone. Because of the large amounts of stock that were involved part of my job consisted of stock control. I was taken to the other side of the building to the stockroom. As I looked around the room my immediate reaction was, "What absolute chaos!" The place was far too small for the large amounts of stock that were being kept and there was only a tiny air vent and no windows. It was hot and stuffy inside. Items of stock were strewn everywhere in a most disorderly fashion. I knew that I would have to re-organize the whole system, as hardly anything tallied with the stock cards. It took most of the week to sort out the items of stock and get some order into the place. I threw the stock cards away and started a ledger. Although my salary was higher than I had previously earned at other companies the increase in workload and responsibility was not worth the extra money that I was earning. I hardly ever finished work before 6.00pm and often, I had to take work home to keep up to date. When I declined invitations to dinner friends commented that it was not fair to my children or me.

It was while I was in the storeroom lugging a huge parcel of goods to be collected by our driver that I suddenly doubled over in the most excruciating pain. I could not straighten up but somehow I managed to get back to my office. All my colleagues stared at me in bewilderment. I was doubled over at a 90 degree angle.

"What happened?" they gasped.

"My back seems to have gone into a spasm," I groaned.

I was helped to a car by one of my colleagues who took me to my doctor. He gave me an injection and prescribed a couple of day's rest in bed. Shortly after my return to work I was moving boxes and once more my back went into a severe spasm. I was again taken to the doctor and he repeated the treatment. Maybe a stronger person's spine could have withstood the weight of the boxes, but mine rebelled.

Ivan questioned me when he saw the condition I was in. "Why are you carrying heavy parcels? Isn't there anyone to help you carry anything at that place? Why do you have to do everything?" He looked worried.

"What can I do? It is part of my job." I replied.

"I don't care whether it is part of your job or not, the company is not going to look after you and your children if you are laid up with your back for life, that I promise you. They will just get someone else. Please be careful."

"You're right," I said sighing.

After this, I had periodic episodes of severe back pain. My doctor sent me to an orthopaedic surgeon who admitted me to hospital and had me put in traction. I was horrified when I saw what the nursing staff were about to do to me. I was bandaged with plaster up to my waist and each leg has seven kilogram weights attached which hung down over pulleys.

Ivan came to visit me regularly, often bringing my boys with him, yet I longed to see all three of my children together. One day I looked out of the window next to my bed and saw all the visitors leaving, including Ivan and my sons, and sighed. I watched them walk to the car. How one takes a simple act like walking for granted, until it is denied! I had always been an active person, moreover a sports enthusiast. Being laid up was extremely frustrating. But the most exasperating part of it was that I was in no position to keep up with my numerous responsibilities. It was a time in my life when I particularly needed to be healthy and energetic. I needed to provide for my children. I needed to participate in their lives so that I could be accepted as a parent once more.

When my spirits were at their lowest that evening something happened which shall be etched in my memory forever. I was alone in the hospital room and it was dark outside. The whole room was filled with a brilliant and pervasive light! The exceeding glory of the light of heaven seemed to fill the place. This supernatural light made me breathless with amazement. I gasped, in awe. I had never seen anything like this before. I suddenly realized I was witnessing the Spirit of the Lord. I knew, then, for certain that He was with me through all my trials and that somehow I would emerge victorious. It was one of the most profound experiences I have ever had. I was so touched by this encounter with the Lord and it encouraged me and strengthened my faith. I knew I was going to be fine although I was not healed at that point.

At last, after what seemed like ages, the ten days passed and the orthopaedic surgeon came to check up on me. I was still in traction with my feet in the air and strapped up.

"There should be a society for cruelty to human beings," I exclaimed.

He grinned.

"You may go home, but I want to see you in two weeks' time."

The nurses came to remove the tractions and plaster. I held on to them as I attempted to walk. After the long period in bed my legs felt like jelly and would hardly carry me. Even though I had been discharged from the hospital I still could not straighten my back and was walking around with a stooped posture. The orthopaedic surgeon finally told me that I needed a spinal fusion and laminectomy but he could only offer me a 45% chance of success. The risk was enormous. I was told that the fusion would give temporary relief but that in a few years the next set of vertebrae might collapse. If there was no flexibility there could be a chain reaction. Furthermore, if the operation was unsuccessful, paralysis could be the result. I was sent home to decide. Within days I had decided against the operation, guided as I was by the Lord's own light. I knew there must be another way. And there was!

Two weeks after I was discharged from the hospital Ivan took me to a church service I was still bent over at an awful angle. Suddenly, a small elderly lady who had been sitting in the pew two rows ahead of me, came up to me and said, "The Lord has told me to pray for you!"

As she laid hands on me and was praying, I claimed the healing. Instantly I felt a heat permeate my body and I straightened. I stood there and realized that I had been healed! Everyone in church looked at me in amazement. One minute I was all bent over and in agony and the next I stood completely straight without the slightest bit of tension or pain. People in the service came rushing up to me overwhelmed with joy at what they had seen.

Arise, go thy way, thy faith hath made thee whole. Luke 17:19

That was my first healing. I could do anything, pick up parcels, run, swim. I was as healthy as most people. I could even go to gym again which was something I enjoyed immensely. Soon I completely forgot that I had ever had back trouble. I went back to the office after my healing and related to my colleagues how I was prayed for and supernaturally healed. Some believed and were amazed and others, the doubters, ascribed my healing to the rest and medication. Soon, I refrained from speaking to people about my healing, being afraid of a rebuff.

Sometime afterwards I decided to visit the previous company for which I had worked. "How is your present employ?" John, my ex-boss asked.

"Pressure," I answered, "more than when I worked for you."

"I warned you," he said. "Some people have to learn the hard way." I said.

"I know, I should have listened, but what's done is done." "By the way, how are the rest of the staff? I inquired. There was a concerned look on his face.

"Stan had a spinal fusion in his cervical region," he said. "It has been unsuccessful and he is unable to use his right arm."

Just then Stan appeared and he seemed to be in a great deal of pain. I looked at him and my heart went out to him. Were it not for the Lord's mercy it could have been my lot.

"Eleanor has recently been hospitalized for her back," John said to Stan.

Stan looked at me and his face was wry with pain as he spoke, "Don't let anyone touch your spine with a scalpel." he said.

I shook my head. "Don't worry, I won't."

When I returned to work that day my duties sent me to the stockroom only to discover that since my hospitalization there had been deliveries and everything had just been dumped in the middle of the room for me to sort out. I had to reorganize the entire stock system from scratch. It was the end of the month and almost three weeks since I had returned to work after my hospital ordeal. I had worked hard to finish my typing and telephonic duties as well as completing the reorganization of the stock.

My boss called me into his office and asked me to take a seat. As I sat down, feeling rather tense, I sensed what he was about to say. "Eleanor," he began, " I am sorry, but we no longer require your services. Here is a letter of termination together with your cheque, giving you two weeks' notice from today." Two weeks' notice! The words hit me. Two weeks was hardly enough time for me to look for another job.

Even though I had anticipated what he was about to say, the words still came as a shock to me. I looked at him, making sure I had eye contact.

He obviously did not enjoy telling me, "Please don't come in for the next two weeks." he added, "We could prefer you not to."

I took the envelope from him, shrugged my shoulders and walked to the elevator. I hadn't even said goodbye to any of my colleagues, and after this, I didn't want to come in again anyway. This was the first time anything like this had happened to me. As I left the building my thoughts raced. I felt certain that I had been given notice because of my back injury. The fact that I had injured myself on duty must have been a strong factor that prompted the company to do away with my services. I could not help feeling resentful; this injury had begun as a result of my efforts to keep their system intact. (A few years later I was to discover that this company had subsequently gone into liquidation, and that the boss who fired me was out of work.)

It was Friday evening and all three children were sitting in the lounge. I told them briefly that I was unemployed.

"Ma has been fired," they chanted.

I shook my head and smiled. They always took the 'mickey' out of me and their humour lightened the situation.

"Perhaps it is a good thing." Ivan responded when I told him. "Just look how exhausted you were from all the pressure. Your back would not have stood up to all that lifting in the storeroom, anyway."

I knew that in a way he was right. But the reality hit me. It was indeed a time of crisis in my life with no employment and no other income. Through all this the Lord was teaching me to commit my way unto Him and to trust Him. Often it is in the darkest hour and the most threatening events that the Lord is nearest to us, ready to deliver.

UNEMPLOYED

Early on Monday morning I went straight to the unemployment office to register. As I approached the building I looked around at the dark grey concrete walls and its cold atmosphere and impersonal gloomy air. My life, it seemed, had become an endless struggle with such institutions since my divorce: schools, companies, hospitals and now finally this. As I entered the building I looked around. There were hundreds of people who were obviously in the same position as me.

I felt humbled that day for I had never had to claim unemployment benefits before. After waiting for what seemed ages I finally managed to register. The unemployment office paid out four fifths of my last salary, which on its own had been hardly enough to live on. I had no savings to fall back on. It was imperative for me to find work. I had registered with many employment agencies but nothing came up. As the weeks went by I started to feel at a low ebb. Finally someone had an interview for me but the work was so far away that it would not have been an economic proposition taking the high travelling costs into account. Then I was offered a job as a representative out in an industrial area. Somehow I did not feel right about the position. It was the prompting of the Spirit of the Lord.

I telephoned a friend. "Do not be hasty El," my friend responded, "I know that this is hard to say to someone in your position, but that company is not even listed in the telephone directory."

She was right. I had to hold on until I found a reputable company. Each Tuesday I had to go and sign the unemployment register. Literally hundreds of people were seated in rows awaiting their turn: women knitting, babies in prams everywhere, middle aged people and young alike, all waiting patiently and hopefully. Soon four months had elapsed. Our situation was desperate. There was only another two months in which I was entitled to draw unemployment benefits. Then what was I going to do? I was the 'breadwinner' in the family.

In South Africa one is only entitled to draw unemployment money for a period of six months during any one period of unemployment. My Christian friends were very supportive at this time, yet I also experienced grave disappointments with people I had respected in the past.

One day I arrived home and the doorbell rang. It was Toni.

"Hello," I said, "What a nice surprise!" I gave her a hug.

She had a couple of carrier bags full of groceries.

"Come in and put your parcels down," I urged.

"This food is for you and the children," she said.

I was speechless. I was about to say I felt embarrassed and that I did not want to take anything from her, but she smiled and cut me short.

"Come on El. You would do the same for me, wouldn't you? What are friends for?"

I hugged her and thanked her in gratitude for the beautiful deed that she had done. Toni was so good to me, frequently inviting me to dinners at her home and really encouraging me. Ethnie, too showed a deep concern for me during these times and prayed with me

A couple of days went by and I was really beginning to feel anxious. There was not much time left in which I could draw unemployment money. Every day I would buy a newspaper to see what jobs were available. The columns were not as long as they used to be. Jobs were scarce. One night, however, something caught my eye. A position was becoming vacant at the Government Department where I had originally been offered a position which, in retrospect, I wished I had accepted. I quickly cut out the advertisement and put it next to the telephone. I was excited, I would definitely apply. Not long after I had submitted my application for the job, I was telephoned to come in for an interview. I was interviewed by a panel of people who all fired questions at me. I answered each question in a calm manner looking straight at the person who had questioned me. When the interview was over I was told that I would have to come back for a second and perhaps a third interview, and that the position was only becoming vacant around mid-January. 'Never mind,' I thought 'it would be worth waiting for as that would be when my unemployment money ended.'

I decided to break off my relationship with Ivan. It wasn't the right time in my life to put a relationship before my children! They need me and I needed them. It was a necessary sacrifice and Ivan, in spite of his strong attachment to me, was very understanding and empathetic. My children came first in my life and their needs although I missed Ivan's friendship and felt a sense of emptiness.

Five months had now elapsed since I lost my job and I only had another month of unemployment money. We were barely making ends meet as it was and I felt that I must find suitable employment before the month ended. I was telephoned to come in for a second interview for the job which I wanted. But they still didn't make their final selection. Shortly after this, Ivan announced that he was going overseas. He had won a trip through the company he worked for as he had done exceptionally well. It was his first overseas trip and I offered to take him to the airport. I was excited for his part as it was a wonderful opportunity and he deserved it. Ivan had given me so much support and affection during some of my most difficult times. It was hard to let go of what had been quite a solid, lasting attachment. Soon time was up and I was standing with him in the departures queue. He kissed me goodbye. Take care while I'm gone, he cautioned. A final announcement cut the air. I did not wait to see the aeroplane take off. I was heart sore about our break-up for a long time afterwards. But I trusted that things would turn out for the better for both of us.

I began to feel on edge again. There were only three weeks left of unemployment money. I decided to take the initiative and telephone the Personnel Section of the Government Department where I had been interviewed. The tension was too much and I could not wait any longer. I had to know one way or the other whether I had a job or not. My mouth was dry with anxiety as I dialled the number. It was the personnel officer who answered. He was the man who had offered me the job originally.

"It's Mrs. Ment," I said, I've just applied for the position as ..... and I was wondering what has happened.

"Just a minute," he answered. "I'll find out for you."

I could hear him dialling another extension. Anxiously I waited. I just had to get that job. I listened to him as he spoke. "The secretarial position for January, has it been filled? I see, thanks."

"Mrs. Ment, I'm awfully sorry to have to tell you this, but the vacancy has already been filled. You will be receiving a letter in the post advising you of this." My heart skipped a beat. I just could not believe it. I was so sure I would be offered the position. I had built my hopes on the job and I was intensely disappointed, The timing would have been just right for I would have begun just when the unemployment benefits ended.

'Somehow I must hold on,' I thought, 'for the Lord is in control of every situation and this seemingly impossible situation will still work out!'

Then I was offered an interview for another job. "

Don't worry Mrs. Ment, it is a reputable company," the agent assured me as I must have sounded a bit dubious when she spoke to me. During the interview I was forewarned that the position was a very pressurized one, that it entailed alternate Saturday morning work and I would without a doubt be expected to work overtime. I knew I just had to take whatever came up. I could not afford to be choosey. I did not like the idea of more pressure because of what had happened in the past but I really had no choice. A couple of days went by. How much longer was I going to wait? And then when I was at the end of my tether, I received a telephone call.

"Is that Mrs. Ment?" It was a lady on the telephone. She was from the Government Department that had turned me down. "The lady that was appointed to the position had decided to stay on in their present job and you are our next choice. Could you come in and we'll send you for a medical examination. If you pass we will liaise with you on a commencement date and you will be sent a letter of appointment, the usual formality." I sighed with relief as I put the telephone down. "Praise the Lord." He was in control and was teaching me to exercise faith and trust Him! At the 11th hour he had supplied my need!

I will never leave thee nor forsake thee. Hebrews 13:5

My three children had gone away on a camp. My flat was so quiet without them. When I was told that I had a position at the Government Department my children arrived home from their holiday camp in the evening.

"Hi Ma," Mervyn said, "my suitcase went missing at the camp!. We looked everywhere for it." A week earlier the loss would have been disastrous, but now it was negligible.

"Never mind," I said, "it's good to see you, and we'll worry about that later." "How was the camp?" I asked.

"Super Ma," Jeremy answered.

"I've got good news, I've been offered a job and have accepted it," I said looking at my childrens' reactions in the rear view mirror as I spoke.

"Ma, we are so glad," they all chanted.

"When are you starting?" "January," I said, "it's the job I wanted."

"Great Ma," Jeremy said. "I'm sure you are all going to head for the bathroom once we get home," I said.

"I'm first," Jeremy said.

"No, I'm going first," Mervyn said.

They looked tired and restless from the long journey and their deeply tanned bodies were covered with sand. Once we arrived home all three dumped their suitcases full of dirty washing in the passage and raced up the stairs to see who could reach the bathroom first.

"Ma I'm starving," Mervyn said.

"Me too," Jeremy said. "How long till supper?"

"Nearly ready," I called grinning. Things were looking up. And it felt wonderful to have all my children home for a change. I had missed them. It felt so good to be involved in motherly chores again. There was such a cold emptiness in the flat when they were gone. I needed them and loved their chatter and laughter. And what is life without children?

RELAPSE

I commenced my duties at my new place of work. On the first day of my job, I surveyed the new surroundings with pleasure. I was in an executive suite. An electronic typewriter was also a joy in those days. I was introduced to the staff and was warmly welcomed. Everyone from the manager to the tea lady had a kind disposition. Everything was just perfect for me. We had a gymnasium in the building. This was for the employees' use and was part of the benefits. Even the meals were subsidized. I loved my job! Soon six months had elapsed. I was settled and enjoying the work immensely. I had almost forgotten that I had ever had back trouble. The weakness was still there, however. Now and again I could feel the sensitivity when I lifted heavy things. Then one weekend I had a relapse. I was scrubbing down tiles in my apartment when I felt the old, sharp, familiar pain.

"Oh no," I groaned. "Not again."

I doubled over and crawled to bed, hoping that the pain would subside before Monday morning. But it didn't. Somehow I managed to get to the office. I was determined not to let my back problem jeopardize my wonderful new job but how I imagined that I was going to do a day's work I just didn't know. People stared at me as I stepped into the lift. I was doubled over at an acute angle, unable to straighten up or even see which floor we had stopped at. Finally I struggled to my desk and sat on the chair. One of my colleagues passing by retraced her steps.

"Hey, what's wrong, girl? You look as if you're in agony." She could see that I was unable to get up from the chair and the pain I was in showed on my face.

"Whew!" she said, "I've never seen anyone with a back as bad as yours. We'd better get you to a doctor." When we arrived the doctor took one look at me and immediately telephoned a neurosurgeon, who said he wanted me admitted to hospital right away. This time there was no facile resorting to an injection.

I telephoned the school my children attended to let the staff know that I was going into hospital, so that they could inform my children of my relapse. Then I contacted a neighbour who kindly promised to break the news to my eldest son when he came home from school. But I was worried. My son Jeremy would soon be writing the matriculation examinations. He didn't need any additional pressures at that critical time.

The surgeon arrived shortly after I had been admitted.

"Now walk," he said, after he had questioned and examined me. Slowly I tried to walk.

"Stand on your toes." he said watching me. "Good, you can get back into bed now, I've seen what I want to see," he said. "I don't think you need any surgery at present; however, I would like a myelogram and X-rays taken just to be certain."

"Whew!" I said. "Thank goodness I escaped the scalpel!"

The following day the radiologist injected dye into my spine and took pictures. One of my colleagues had warned me about a myelogram.

"Don't lie flat for about 18 hours afterwards," she warned.

I remembered those words when I was finally taken back to my ward and promptly placed a pile of cushions behind me. My bed had been wound up into a sitting position. I sat upright for a couple of hours. One of the sisters noticed this.

She said, "You've just had a myelogram, haven't you?" I nodded. She said, "Let's see if we can't make you more comfortable."

She wound the bed down until it was level again. "There now! That's better isn't it?"

I lay flat on my back and stared at the ceiling, a little confused however about the contradiction between my friend's advice and that of the sister. The neurosurgeon came to see me that evening. Taking a look at my pictures methodically he said, "You have a prolapsed disc between L5 and L4 and scoliosis is evident. There is nothing touching any important centres at the moment; no operation is necessary at this stage. However, you may need a spinal fusion later on." (The Orthopaedic Surgeon had recommended a fusion prior to my first healing.)

The side- effect of the myelogram were debilitating. About half an hour after the neurosurgeon had left, I began to feel terribly sick. I thought my head was going to burst with the pain and I was vomiting uncontrollably. The nurse tried to hold my head over the kidney bowl for I could not sit upright. Everything was spinning around me. I was given an injection which relieved the pain and induced sleep. The following morning I was desperate to go home. I thought of two possible people who might fetch me. Inch by inch I eased myself off the bed and began a slow walk down the long corridor to the call box. I was so light-headed that people and objects seemed to float away from me as I approached them. Eventually I could not bear the stabbing pain and dizziness. I lay down in the corridor. Wet with perspiration I managed to crawl to the telephone and heave myself up. The one friend I phoned said she was sick and the other was out. In desperation I phoned my local pharmacist. He was there within minutes. It was such a relief to leave that depressing hospital and to know that I had escaped the operating table. Eventually the side effects subsided. At least they had located the source of my back problem and with the short rest my back had readjusted to a relatively stable condition allowing me to resume work again. It was a relief to be with my colleagues again in my work environment and to be reunited at home with my children and out of hospital.

God's love does not keep us from trials – it helps us get through them.

THE LORD PROVIDES

But they that wait upon the Lord shall renew their strength; they shall mount up with wings as eagles; they shall run and not be weary; and they shall walk and not faint. Isaiah 40:31

Jeremy was due to attend University the following year. I was worried as to how I was going to pay for this. Student loans were hard to obtain for first year students because of the high 'drop out' rate and bursaries were also difficult to obtain. I acquired a list of all the bursaries which were available and applied to three Universities on his behalf.

I was enjoying my exercise classes so much that I decided to enrol for a teacher's course. I could manage to study part-time now that my job was not so demanding. I was required to study all the theory first and then do the practical the following year. Part-time lectures were held at the University twice a week in the evenings and I had to study six subjects: anatomy, physiology, psychology, nutrition, biomechanics and business administration. I was especially motivated to study because Jeremy intended doing medicine the following year and I didn't know how I was going to finance this. It would be a pity for him to do his military training before proceeding to University. It is invariably more difficult to get back to the routine of studying once one has had such a long break. I intended running an exercise/weight-control group once a week in the evenings which would be an extra income to subsidise Jeremy. I was excited and organized a venue well in advance. All the courses involved just what I had always been interested in. Most of our lecturers had Ph.D degrees in their particular fields and had a wealth of knowledge to impart. It entailed at least three hours of study every night to keep up-to-date. Jeremy was studying hard for the matriculation examinations and would often say to me 'Come on Ma, get down to some studying.'

He loved reading and studying so much that when he was a child I nick-named him the 'bookworm'. He was such an encouragement to me. I so enjoyed the lectures that I really didn't mind sitting with my books and notes in the evenings and during weekends. I was now doing as many as three gym classes a day. I was to learn later when I did Physiology that exercise increased the endorphin level in the brain which is a morphine-like substance and that one can become addicted to it. Well, I certainly was. I was usually up at 5.15am and arrived at the gym at 6.00am for the early morning class with my working clothes and shoes etc. After exercise classes I had a swim and showered. I felt so alive, refreshed and alert to concentrate on my day's work. At lunch time I would do another class and sometimes on my way home from work I would either do the circuit or a further class which meant that on average I was doing the equivalent of three classes a day.

"Three classes a day is crazy," one of the ladies said to me at the gymnasium. "You are really addicted."

I just grinned. "I can think of far worse things to become addicted to," I replied.

The orthopaedic surgeon had advised me to exercise in order to keep my muscles flexible. I never considered the possibility that I might be overdoing it with my history of back problems.

We were given our examination timetable and told that if we failed or were unable to attend the finals, due to ill health or a business commitment, a supplementary examination could be written in March of the following year. The following Saturday I was up early and busy with my household chores. I was feeling a bit nervous, after all it was some time since I had last written examinations. I was in the kitchen and had switched the kettle on. As I turned around to switch it off I felt the old familiar pain in my back again. I managed to walk to my bedroom to lie down. I was so disappointed. I could not understand it. Here I was doing gym classes three times a day and performing exercises which virtually flexed every muscle and joint in my body with no ill-effects and now a simple twisting around to switch off the kettle put my back out of joint again. It seemed as if I was prone to inexplicable relapses. My fellow students, who had arrived for our study session that afternoon, had looks of dismay on their faces when they saw my condition.

"Eleanor, you will be far better off with a spinal fusion," one of them concluded.

"Well if I can do without that operation I will," I replied. "Besides the chances of success are probably not that high with the scoliosis which is evident on my X-rays. Anyway, I will have some rest in bed this weekend and I'm sure that I'll be O.K. for the examination on Monday."

However, when it came to Monday I was no better. I was still doubled over when we arrived at the hall.

"You should leave the examinations and write a supplementary next year," one of the students suggested.

"A winner never quits." I said and managed a smile.

I was given a glass of water and two pain killers. We all began writing and there was absolute silence in the hall. The examination paper was a multiple choice. Some of the questions were tricky and it was hard for me to concentrate, for I was in a great deal of pain. However, I managed to finish on time and handed in my paper.

"Your condition will be taken into account," the lecturer remarked.

"What is the problem with your spine?" "The diagnosis was a prolapsed disc and scoliosis," I answered.

"Go and see Dr. ....., he runs a clinic and specializes in people with back problems," he suggested.

Shortly after I had written my examinations I had to return to the hospital for more rest and treatment. My lecturer had been so pleased with my results that he rushed to the hospital to tell me of my achievement. I had, however, been discharged in the interim. When I heard that he had gone to the hospital to tell me, I was disappointed at missing him and telephoned him immediately. He congratulated me and said that my mark was 83%. I knew that the pass mark was 50%, but I also knew that I had missed the merit award by 3%.

'Great,' I thought, 'I can't wait to tell the children.'

My results were in the letter box shortly afterwards. When I arrived home, Jeremy was sitting at the dining room table and studying. Grinning widely, I placed the letter with the results in front of him.

"Who said I wouldn't pass?" I asked.

Jeremy smiled back at me. "Well done ma," he said.

On Tuesday, graduation day, I drove out to the medical school in time to find a seat near the front row. The hall was packed with students and their families. I thought wistfully how nice it would be if one of the children had been there to see me. Just then Toni caught my eye as she entered the door and I knew that she had come especially to see me graduate. I gave her a hug and thanked her for her support. After the merit awards were handed out the lecturer called me up to collect my certificate: "Eleanor deserved a special applause as she was quite ill when she wrote her exams." I beamed at his words. I felt like a proud child again. That evening I sighed as I placed my certificate next to my dressing table. I felt a real sense of achievement as I examined all the subjects that were listed. It just shows what can be accomplished with a little effort and the Lord's help even when the odds are against you.

Soon Jeremy was writing his first matriculation examination. I could not believe that he was old enough to write his 'matric'. I wished him all the best as I dropped him at the hall where he was to write. He was very nervous; A lot depended on his results as he had his heart set on studying medicine. After work that evening I rushed home eager to find out how he had found his first paper. In spite of his headache, it seemed to have gone well. I took a look around Jeremy's room while we were talking. His matriculation timetable was stuck to the wall. At the bottom of the timetable he had written in large letters - FREE. I smiled as I read it. Soon all the tension would be over. Jeremy had been through so many of my own troubles with me, not to mention all the stress related to his own aspirations. He really deserved to achieve his goals.

"Come on," I said, "I'll make you a bite to eat."

"Ma, I'm just not hungry at the moment," he said.

"You should eat, that's probably why you have such a headache."

But he was adamant. Whenever he was under a lot of stress he lost his appetite. Soon Jeremy had finished writing the last of his examinations. The matriculation results were already on the computer at the university which was linked up with the Department of Education. In Cape Town it was extremely difficult to get into Medical School even if you had the money. We had nothing, and loans were unavailable for first year students. Bursaries were almost impossible to obtain.

Shortly after Jeremy left for a three week holiday camp the results came through. I bought the newspaper and eagerly paged through the many columns to search for Jeremy's results. He had not only passed but done exceptionally well. As soon as I arrived home I telephoned the camp as he had asked me to do. The line was bad for it was a long distant call and it took ages before he came to the telephone.

"Jeremy, it's mom, how are you?"

"I'm fine Ma," he replied. "Guess what!" I exclaimed, "You obtained an A symbol for maths."

"You're kidding," he replied, "Great! Ma."

He was pleased but after a short silence he asked if there had been any news from Medical School, and I had to tell him that I'd heard nothing. When camp was over he arrived home only to press the same question and again I had to tell him that there was no news. He was terribly disappointed.

In the meantime my back had improved and I advertised my exercise and weight/control classes in the local newspapers. Toni came to the hall to give me a hand and I began eagerly writing notes on the board in preparation for the class. I was excited for I had had numerous responses to the advertisement. However, only two people arrived and I was very disappointed. Toni tried to persuade me that it would take a while to catch on and that people would advertise by word of mouth, but I was inconsolable. I was certain that Jeremy would be accepted into Medical School and I had started these classes specifically to raise the funds for his course. The following week I had four people and soon a few more came, but it was still not sufficient. Eventually I decided to throw in the towel. It did not pay me to hire a hall for so few people. Jeremy was becoming anxious as the university term approached.

"I needn't have worked so hard for my matric," he exclaimed, "I was accepted for a Bachelor of Science degree before I even wrote matric, but that's not what I want to do." "Hold on, Jeremy," I said, "I'm praying for you and I'm sure you'll be accepted."

. He was so afraid of being disappointed. He had set his heart on medicine. It was a profession that really suited him, not only because he was intelligent, but because he was a caring considerate person and he was level-headed enough to cope with the psychological pressures. I found lovely lodgings for Jeremy near the university, even though there was still no news from Medical School – I was doing this in faith.

Then a few days later, while I was deeply engrossed in my work at the office I received a telephone call from the Medical School. He had been accepted. I was elated. I made such a commotion that all my bosses come rushing out of their offices. I immediately telephoned Jeremy.

"You'll never guess what," I said to him on the phone."

"What? Quickly, don't leave me guessing," he replied. "You've been accepted by the Medical School."

"Wonderful!" he replied with youthful enthusiasm. "You've made my day."

Soon Jeremy was settled into his lodgings and his new routine at university. He had an interview for a bursary lined up, but I still lay awake at night worrying about how I was going to finance his studies. I need not have been concerned. The Lord is in control of everything.

One morning I was telephoned while I was a work and informed that the bursary for Jeremy had been granted. I was overjoyed. Apparently someone had passed away and left money in trust for a medical student in need. A few weeks later Jeremy told me that he had received two more bursaries from the university. There was more than sufficient funds for Jeremy's entire years at Medical School. Not only were the bursaries sufficient for Jeremy's Medical studies but they paid for all his books and his student accommodation. I need not have worried. The Lord had provided for everything so beautifully. If only I had waited on Him. I had seen how implicitly the Lord could be trusted even in dire extremity.

PART 3

THE NEAR FATAL INJECTION

Since I was still suffering intermittent pains in the lumbar region of my spine, I decided to contact the specialist who had been recommended to me for another opinion. I took my myelogram pictures with me and related the history of my ailment.

"I can give you an injection to relieve the pain if you like. It contains cortisone and has an anaesthetic effect. Are you in agreement?"

"Sure," I said, trustingly.

I watched him as he filled the large syringe with fluid. He than injected it into my spine. It took ages to administer and he sat on a stool next to me while the fluid was going in. Then he wrote out a prescription for a steel brace to support my back. The injection gave me a measure of relief at first, but after a few days the pain became even more intense and overwhelming than before. I could not understand why it had this contrary effect. If only I had known the repercussions of that injection! Shortly after this I received the account from the specialist. I looked at the account and was horrified to read the words 'epidural pain block injection.' 'Epidural? Why had the doctor administered an epidural?' I had heard of women in labour being given an epidural but never for back problems.

'Oh well,' I thought and shrugged my shoulders, putting the account to one side and not giving it another thought. One is led to have implicit faith in doctors. My condition progressively deteriorated. One morning in early February 1985, when I stepped out of bed to get dressed for work, I was in absolute agony with my back. Any pain I had had prior to this was nothing in comparison to the excruciating agony which I now experienced. The pain was no longer localized in the area where I had felt it up to now; it had become all pervasive and had spread down through my legs. My eyes were rolling back from the intensity of the pain and walking was absolute agony. Each time I took a step it jarred my spine. Somehow I managed to drag myself to my G.P.'s surgery after work.

He took one look at me and shook his head. "You'll have to be booked into hospital right away."

"Oh no!" I protested, "I'm sick of hospitals!"

I telephoned one of my bosses on the following day to inform him that the doctors wanted me to be admitted to hospital again." He said that I had better have the treatment. He was a very sensitive man. I sighed in response but I knew he was right. It was now the fourth time that I had been admitted to hospital with my back problem.

I was examined later by the neurosurgeon, the one who had admitted me previously and had requested a myelogram. He didn't know that I had, in the interim, seen another specialist who had administered an epidural injection to me. I didn't think it was necessary to tell him, as the injection had been administered merely for pain relief. It was not as if I had been under different treatment. The neurosurgeon requested a computerized tomography (C.T. scan).This machine was new in South Africa at the time. It was the latest in modern equipment and did not subject the patient to high doses of radiation. The scan was to be done at another hospital and the sister suggested that I arrange my own transport. I managed to get to a public call-box to telephone two friends but they were both out.

'Oh well,' I thought, 'my motor car is readily available.' (I had been taken to the hospital in my car by a colleague, a second colleague had followed in his car and they had left my vehicle in the hospital parking bay.)

My legs felt like jelly and I was hardly able to drive. I took a look at myself in the rear-view mirror. My face had lost most of its colour and my cheeks were sunken.

"You look awfully pale," the receptionist remarked on my arrival. "Did someone bring you?"

I shook my head, "I drove here myself." I didn't feel much like going into any detail.

"We have an ambulance on call, if the situation ever arises again," she replied.

I thanked her and said that I would bear this in mind if the need should arise again. The radiologist conducted the C.T. scan and handed me my X-rays:

"I phoned your specialist and he said I must tell you to drive carefully back to the hospital and he'll meet you there to discuss the scan. Your doctor may want to compare the scan with your myelogram pictures," he said before I left.

What an ordeal! I had to fetch the latter from my home. I had to go through the whole procedure three times, trying to drive the car when I could hardly sit up straight. When I finally returned to the hospital I discovered that I had missed my appointment with the specialist. He had already left to do his hospital visitations. I was somewhat upset to say the least. I was anxious to know the results of the scan so I phoned my G.P. later and told him what had happened.

"Never mind", he reassured me, "Dr ..... discussed the results of the scan with me. I have good news for you, the scan revealed a disc lesion and you may go home. Yet in spite of his hastiness and optimism I was advised to wear my steel brace day and night to support my spine. I could not understand why the pain was still so intense when the doctors had so casually dismissed me.

Jeremy lived at his lodgings an hour's drive away and was under pressure with his studies. There was no one available to help me get around doing my chores. My younger children stayed with friends while my back injury persisted and I was in constant pain.

At first I tried, with great difficulty, to drive myself around. One afternoon as I was reversing out of a parking bay the engine cut out. I couldn't turn around to reverse properly because of the steel brace. The driver behind me started hooting as I was holding him up. I didn't have the strength to turn the steering wheel and soon more drivers were hooting. Eventually I just broke down and began to cry. One of the driver's realized that something was wrong and came to my assistance and reversed my car out for me. It was so humbling to have to receive help in mundane tasks that other people take for granted every moment of their lives. Three days had elapsed since my hospitalization and I felt I would go crazy just lying around at home all the time. Still I was determined to go back to the office the next day, in spite of the pain. I needed the mental stimulation of my work. My colleagues welcomed me back but were shocked at my condition and at the weight I had lost.

"You look terrible," one of them said, "You should not be at work in your condition. You can hardly walk."

They requisitioned a special chair for me which took the pressure off my spine and placed it on the knees. My boss came out of his office to check if my new chair was suitable.

"What must I do with my other chair?" I asked him. "Oh, we'll keep that for the next secretary," he teased, grinning.

"Maybe she'll fall pregnant like my predecessor." I said jokingly. At least I had not lost my sense of humour.

Each morning my neighbours took turns to carry me down the stairs, drive me to work and help me onto the escalator. One such morning I was holding tightly onto the rail as the escalator was ascending when a tall, heavily built man two steps ahead of me lost his balance. I watched with horror as he fell backwards against me. I, in turn, fell against the people behind me which resulted in quite a pile-up on the escalator. The crushing weight of people on top of me jarred my spine and the pain became almost unbearable. I was carried to the ground floor and one of the staff was called to drive me home. The benefits of my rest in bed were now totally undone. I was in excruciating pain. My back was so frail and sensitive that the slightest bump or jolt was debilitating. Nevertheless I continued to drag myself to work. One day at the office I received a phone call from the Security Services:

"Mrs. Ment, we have been advised that you are disabled and, in the case of an evacuation of the building, we want to ensure that you be taken to safety in one of the lifts." I was stunned . . . the word disabled hit me like a sledgehammer. I just could not face the reality of my condition. It was true, I was virtually a cripple. I couldn't even sit for any length of time, it was too painful and I would have to lie down intermittently on the couch. As I struggled to get into my office one morning a lady remarked that I might as well be in a wheelchair. I just couldn't cope with a day's work. Out of desperation I decided to see my G.P. again. When he saw the state I was in he looked worried and was defensive.

"My patients usually get better," he remarked. He contacted the neurosurgeon and I was again admitted to hospital and put in skin traction for ten days. My colleagues and my bosses empathized with my situation and were really concerned about me.

"We just want to see you be your old cheerful self again," one of my colleagues said when he came to fetch me.

I phoned my boss to ask him if there was anything I could do from home. "No," he said kindly, "just get better!"

I was still receiving a full salary as I had a bit of leave due to me. After that, my boss had agreed to give me unpaid leave. I would then receive sick benefits from the Department of Manpower, though the amount was meagre.

My physical weakness had, by now, started affecting me both mentally and emotionally. I began to experience tremendous psychological depression because I could no longer cope with the simplest and most mundane of tasks. A couple of days had elapsed since my fifth hospitalization, and I had to go shopping for groceries. My three children were coming home for the weekend. The five minute walk to the Superstores took ages. People stared at me as I attempted to walk. I looked exactly like one of those wind-up dolls. My steel brace supported my spine, but I was terrified someone would bump into me in the Superstores because of what had happened previously. There was an empty trolley available but I was unable to push it. I was at the fruit stand trying to reach for some fruit. I turned in desperation to a lady standing next to me.

"I'm sick, could you please help me?" I said

She shrugged : "I'm also sick."

I took a look at her. She did seem to have a slight cold. I felt like telling her that at least she could walk but I said nothing. Then I saw an acquaintance I had known for years.

"Harry," I called. He looked at me in dismay.

"What happened," he asked. "You were always so well."

He seemed upset at seeing me like this, and shook his head in disbelief. He helped me pack the trolley and place it in the queue for me. I thanked him, and then he said he was sorry he could not help me any further as he had another urgent commitment. I held on to the trolley and began to pray.

"Oh Lord, please help me," I cried

I was standing in the queue feeling claustrophobic and terrified someone would bump into me when I eventually broke down and collapsed on the floor. The staff rushed to my assistance and the manager was extremely kind. He took my trolley to the front of the checkout and led me to a corner where no one could bump me. I was driven home by one of the staff.

Before I left the Superstore the manager said: "Whenever you need groceries, please phone us and we will deliver them to your home. You can't go out in that condition."

Shortly after the Superstores ordeal, it was my birthday. I decided to treat myself to a new hairdo and persuaded my neighbour to drive me to the salon. I remember being unable to open the door of the salon. The lady kept beckoning me to enter, signalling constantly until finally she realized that I could not negotiate the door. I felt as if there were endless glass doors between myself and healthy ordinary people. I was having to come to terms with being completely helpless. For someone who was used to hopping in and out of the car and driving everywhere, I now had to rely completely on other people. When I arrived home I was met by Agnes, the charlady who worked for me. She was marvellous. Even though she was employed as a cleaning lady she zealously assumed other responsibilities during those difficult times, helping me to dress, opening drawers for me, helping me to perform all the ordinary little chores of everyday living. Her function had changed from domestic servant to that of a full-time nurse. Agnes was a Christian and a regular church-goer.

"I'm going to pray that you get better, madam," she constantly reassured me, as she bustled around the apartment.

I felt like a prisoner in my own apartment. I could do little but lie in bed. I was soon little more than bedridden. As the days went on, my thoughts raced and I began to feel panicky. Frantically I wondered what I was going to do for money for I would be unable to resume work when my unpaid leave expired in a few weeks' time. Due to my short service with my employers there was very little pension money owing to me. A policy I had taken out which covered accident and disability had lapsed because I could no longer afford to keep up the payments. Up to then we had lived solely on the salary I earned and I had absolutely no savings left.

In desperation I decided to telephone the neurosurgeon that had attended to me. Up to that stage, I had not mentioned that I had gone to another specialist for a second opinion and received an epidural injection for pain relief. The neurosurgeon was shocked and perplexed when I told him of this.

"Who gave you that injection?" he asked in a tone of disbelief.

He immediately sent me to the head of the orthopaedic section at a provincial hospital for more intensive tests. On my arrival I was placed on a stretcher to begin a long wait. As it was a provincial hospital one did not receive the VIP treatment one does at a private institution. Eventually I was seen by the head of the department. He questioned me in detail about the history of my back complaint. He then telephoned the neurosurgeon and they discussed me around the corner from where I lay. I began to get anxious, wondering what was really wrong with me. I wished the surgeons would tell me what they thought instead of leaving me in suspense. The orthopaedic surgeon at the provincial hospital then examined me using a series of sensitivity tests. He gently pricked a pin into my skin at various points from my waist down to my legs to test my response. I couldn't feel the pin prick in some of the areas he tested. When he tried to raise my left leg it hardly moved and I couldn't push against his hand when he asked me to do so.

After the examination the orthopaedic surgeon said that he wanted a fresh set of X-rays and that I was to see him afterwards. My thoughts raced. Something was seriously wrong with me which meant I could be subjected to more radiation. Sometime after that I had more X-rays taken. As I lay waiting on a stretcher in the corridor, the neurosurgeon hastily appeared. He was an extremely busy man. I wondered why the head of the department of orthopaedics had called him away from his consulting rooms to the hospital. The two surgeons again discussed me, for what seemed like ages. Eventually they called me into the office. The orthopaedic surgeon looked at me gravely.

"You've got to accept this," Mrs. Ment. "There is nerve root involvement and important centres in your back are affected." "We have a pain clinic to help ease your pain and a psychiatric clinic to help you to accept your condition. You haven't got a disc lesion and a fusion wouldn't help in your particular case."

I could not believe it. Everything the doctors had told me up to now had been invalid and inconclusive. I felt utterly confused and alone; there was obviously nothing more the doctors could do for me. Even a wheelchair would not be an aid, for at this stage, I could not sit because of the pressure on a nerve root. I had to either kneel or lie down. When I arrived home I immediately telephoned a friend and related to her what the orthopaedic surgeon had said.

She confirmed my fears. "There's definitely something serious that they are not telling you," she said.

As we were discussing my condition it occurred to us that the probable cause of my suffering was the Epidural injection. The orthopaedic surgeon, too, had been horrified when he heard about the injection. Semi-paralysis must have set in as a result of the Epidural. Yet both surgeons never once stated clearly that this could have been the cause.

I sighed - I would have to strengthen my faith and cry out to the Lord. There was no place to turn, no-one to turn to. Only God remained. And in the moment of crisis that was my only hope. No longer would I trust in my own understanding. No longer would I depend and rely on others. Deep down I began to realize that where all else had failed the Lord would heal me. Faith sees the invisible, believes the incredible and claims the impossible!

MY HEALING

Six horrible months elapsed during which time I was totally bed-ridden. I could not be moved from my bed and Agnes had to help wash me. Many of my friends turned away from me at this time. Perhaps they could not face the condition I was in. Agnes frequently dialled the number of one of my closest friend and held the telephone for me. I pleaded with her to visit me, but even she came up with excuses to avoid me. She did not visit me once.

One afternoon as I lay despairing in my lonely apartment, Ethnie, the elderly lady I had met at church, came to pray for me. As she prayed for me, she had a vision of my being healed and made whole again. It was as if she had thrown me a life-belt and somehow I knew that the Lord was going to heal me. It was like awakening from a nightmare to a world of light and hope. Ruth, my colleague, had watched me gradually deteriorate with concern and compassion. She contacted a couple by the name of Victor and Betty Graham who conducted a healing ministry. It was the 7th July 1986 when they came to see me. That evening I heard a knock at my door

. "Come in," I shouted, "It's open!"

"Hello," Victor said as he walked in. "Now Eleanor, tell me exactly what is wrong with you?"

"My back. I have a degenerative spine and now I'm bed-ridden. The doctors have given up on me."

"Well it's nothing that the Lord cannot heal," Victor said. "Believe me, we are going to see a miracle.

Man's adversity is God's opportunity."

"Is there anyone you haven't forgiven," Betty asked. "If so, release that person to the Lord before we pray."

I nodded. In humility of heart and acute brokenness of spirit I saw the need of repentance before the Lord. This was the beginning of an essential task and I instinctively knew that my healing depended on it. There was anger and bitterness in my heart and I had to let go of it all and forgive. I confessed out aloud and forgave those whom I reproached in my heart.

Victor had some oil with him and anointed me with it. Then they took turns to pray over me for some time. After Betty and Victor had finished praying for me they sat next to my bedside and spoke to me at length. I told them my two younger children were staying with friends as I could not cope while in this condition and they prayed for us to be reunited as a family.

"Be sure to let us know how you are," Victor said. With that the couple left.

After that I slowly began to regain my strength. Each day I tried to walk. At first I looked like a stiff-jointed doll. I looked exactly like a spinal fusion patient the day they start walking after the operation. It was a terrible sight and people used to stare at me as I attempted to walk. Gradually my limbs were freed and it was as though a heavy weight on my back was being lifted. I had to concentrate on those people in my life whom I had to learn to forgive. I had to forgive the Jewish community, including my own family, for initially rejecting me because of my Christian beliefs. I had to forgive the firm that had fired me because of my back injury.

I just said, Lord, I release this person to you, I die to those hurts, and gradually all the suppressed anger in me subsided and I began to be healed. I still wore a brace for a while but my back was getting stronger. It took a long time before I was walking perfectly normally again. In fact, it was a whole year and a half before my healing was complete. From when my back injury started and deteriorated it took one and a half years and the whole episode of my back injury to my complete healing took an entire three years.

At this stage I was able to resume my work on an intermittent basis. When I had about 80% healing and I was being helped on with my brace one morning the Lord impressed on me to get rid of the steel brace I was wearing. Now this huge steel brace had become a physical part of me, it supported my whole spine. I was petrified of walking without it. On this particular morning the Lord clearly indicated to me that He wanted me to get rid of the brace and to trust Him implicitly. I cannot describe in words what I experienced in taking that step in faith, but somehow the Lord strengthened my faith and I threw the brace away.

From then on my complete healing began. When my father saw how I had recovered he was amazed.

"The Lord must be with you," he said. "This could only have been a miracle."

Those were wonderful words coming from an Orthodox Jew. Just before I was due back at the office again, I had to go to the superstore where I had collapsed one year earlier. Some of the staff came rushing up to me, amazed at the sprightly way I was walking. I then saw the same acquaintance who had helped pack my trolley and place it in the queue when I was hardly able to walk. "Hello Harry," I said smiling. "You're walking!" he exclaimed in amazement. "How did it come right? Was it the physiotherapist or the doctors? Did you receive any specific treatment?" I smiled as I watched him try to rationalize the wonderful transformation he saw in me. I shook my head. "Just prayer," I said, " I've been supernaturally healed. I am a walking proof of the healing power of the Lord Jesus Christ and I praise Him for my healing."

One Saturday, almost eighteen months after my healing, I bumped into Victor and Betty Graham (the couple who had a healing and deliverance ministry). Just imagine their faces when I walked up to say 'hello.' They had not actually seen me since I was bed-ridden, and I was not only walking normally but I was carrying parcels as well! They were so excited to see me so well. The Lord had brought people into my pathway who had previously witnessed me unable to walk and who now saw me walking normally again. Literally hundreds of people witnessed this absolute miracle with their own eyes. All my colleagues at the office were talking about my miraculous healing.

My two younger children came home as I was able to look after them. What a joy to be reunited as a family once more!

Moreover, I was in the position now more than ever before to provide for my children, both financially and emotionally. I had to make many sacrifices but I did so happily and willingly. I hardly went out, for I spent all my spare time with Mervyn and Amy, more so than ever before.

They were so pleased to be home once more and would come with me to the Superstores and enjoyed helping me select the groceries. Amy would make supper for us and I would arrive home from work to find the table laid and a cooked meal prepared. Soon a whole year had gone by and all the unpleasant memories started to fade away while at the same time a process of emotional healing was taking place. What was behind was behind! Never before had the children and I appreciated each other as much as we did now. We were more than just family. We had become close friends.

THE FRUITS OF MY HEALING

I will repay you for the years the locusts have eaten – the great locust and the young locust and the other locusts and the locust swarm – My great army that I sent among you. You will have plenty to eat, until you are full, and you will praise the name of the Lord your God, who has worked wonders for you; never again will my people be ashamed. Then you will know that I am in Israel, that I am the Lord your God   Joel 2:25-27 NIV

It was now nearly three years since my miraculous healing had taken place. Every aspect of my life was running smoothly. In fact, my healing involved more than just a physical recovery. Through the experience I was rejuvenated and replenished on the emotional and spiritual levels as well. My children too were reaping the rewards of the hard trials they had endured in the past. Jeremy had by now almost completed his third year at Medical School and was doing exceptionally well. Amy had received a prize for the top student at College and Mervyn was about to write his matriculation examinations and had done well in the preliminaries. I was particularly pleased, for in spite of all we had been through as a family, the children had matured in their own ways and they were achieving in their particular fields.

Jeremy was now 20 years of age, 6 ft tall and good looking. He had turned into a level headed young man, studious and very knowledgeable about world affairs. He had always been an exceptional achiever, and moreover, he was willing to share his knowledge by teaching others. He had always been a very considerate person. I remember one day noticing how his shoes were worn and full of holes. I asked him why he had not told me.

"Ma, I know how you're struggling with your finances. I didn't want to add another worry."

Mervyn was almost as tall as Jeremy, slender and good looking. He had an athletic build and the most beautiful blue-green eyes. He always had a very sociable disposition. Often if the telephone rang, Mervyn would say "Ma, don't bother to answer, it's not for you," and sure enough it would be a young lady wanting to speak to him. He loved going to parties and being on the beach with his pals. He managed to get through school by rarely opening a book. He preferred sport, and indeed he excelled at soccer and athletics at provincial level. Amy was the shortest of us all at 5 ft 4 in and her lovely thick brown hair hung down to her waist. She looked gorgeous with her flawless complexion and I was proud of her responsible attitude. She was responsible and would telephone whenever she visited a friend to let me know where she was. Amy had a warm, generous nature, always spending her savings on gifts for others. She was quite content to be at home, skilful at cooking and baking and displaying a flair for decorating. Often I would arrive home to find a special dinner which Amy had prepared for us. I was delighted at how my three children had grown up and I was extremely proud of them.

Moreover I was, and still am, eternally grateful every day for my physical health. Being the same active and energetic person again has given me a chance to join my children in their sport and recreation. It is important to me that we are now able to share and celebrate the joy of our togetherness with full enthusiasm.

Jeremy decided to stay with my parents in Sea Point when he was home from university. He found it much easier to study at my parents' apartment where there was no one to distract him. My parents were getting on in years. My father was 78 years old and still doing translations for companies to keep him occupied. He still had a very active mind. Mom had turned 73 and looked very attractive for her age. They were overjoyed at having Jeremy stay with them and they made quite a fuss of him.

Since the writing of this book Eleanor has retained her healing for more than 30 years. Jeremy is a qualified medical heart surgeon in England, Mervyn is living in London, managing his own restaurants and Amy, living in Israel. All three children are happily married. In spite of all what the family has endured, they are all doing exceptionally well. Abe died of a heart attack on 6th December 1989.

Two years after Mervyn and Amy had come home our landlord decided to renovate the block of apartments where we had stayed for seven years. Mervyn and Amy were keen to move to Sea Point as all their friends were there. Sea Point is a lovely area in Cape Town with stretches of beaches along the coast.

One day as I was driving to visit my parents and Jeremy, I saw a sign saying 'Show Flat'. I followed the sign and walked into the most beautifully renovated duplex apartment. It was an absolute delight with a tiny staircase leading up into the living quarters and a beautifully tiled bathroom. A shower would be such a luxury for me, especially after what I had been through with my back injury. It was within walking distance of my parent's residence. I took Mervyn and Amy to have a look and they immediately expressed their delight. They adored the place. After I had spoken to the agent I went straight to the Housing Loans Section at work. My firm guaranteed the bond and with the housing subsidy it worked out that my repayments would be no more than what I was paying for my existing accommodation. The transfer costs were also added on to the bond and so I did not have to lay out a single cent. Soon the time came for us to move and Mervyn and Amy were so excited. They each had their own bedroom overlooking the sea. It was so wonderful to be able to provide for their needs and wishes after all the struggles. And it was a blessing to live in a more attractive, homely environment. For so many years I had battled to provide the basic essentials for our survival.

After my healing I began to feel a profound spiritual change in me. There was no need anymore to be obsessed with worldly things: money, shelter and food. I was blessed now with the freedom to focus on the spiritual dimension of my life. And as I became more eternity-minded and spiritually stronger I found the opportunity to give to others in a way that I had never been able to before.

Three days after we had moved into our new apartment I took a walk to see my parents and Jeremy. I rang the door bell and my mother came to the door. She looked worried.

"What's wrong?" I asked concerned. "Dad's ill," she said, "he's complaining of a swollen leg."

"Mom, I'm sure it can't be much," I said. "Don't worry, where is Dad, can I see him?" Mom nodded and led the way to their bedroom. There Dad lay, with his leg elevated, looking rather pale.

"Hello Dad," I said. "What's wrong?" "I'm in a bit of pain," he said. His face showed the intensity of the pain he was in. I knew then that it was serious for I had never heard Dad complain before.

After spending some time with Dad and giving him a verse of scripture from the Old Testament to read, I left feeling uneasy.

"Oh Lord," I prayed on the way home, "Please let me have an opportunity to speak to my Dad on my own about You."

It was shortly after this that the Lord granted this. I was at work and the telephone rang, it was Mom.

"Eleanor, Dad is at the hospital being X-rayed, please can you fetch him?" "Sure Mom," I said. "What time?"

"Don't know," she said, "I'll give you the hospital number and you can ring them yourself."

"Leave it to me," I said. "I'll fetch Dad."

At about 6.30 p.m. I drove to the hospital. There was Dad waiting for me at the elevators. I took his arm and helped him slowly to the car.

"When will you have the results?"

"Probably within a day or so," he said.

As I was driving him home, I began witnessing to him.

"Dad," I said, "it's either heaven or hell, there is no middle path. You either accept the Lord Jesus Christ or you reject Him. But if you reject Him you won't go to heaven when you die. You have to verbally say, Lord Jesus I acknowledge you as my Lord and Saviour, forgive me for my sins and I ask you to take control of my life."

Dad never said a word to me as I was driving home. He just listened as I spoke. I wished deeply that my words would have the power to commit on his behalf. When I arrived at the flat I helped him inside and Mom put him straight to bed. I had phoned a Christian friend beforehand and she had been interceding for my Dad while he and I were alone in the car. She phoned me the next day to say she felt in her spirit that Dad had received the gospel. A couple of days later when I went to see my parents, Dad related to me that the X-rays revealed a tumour which was pressing against the arteries and causing the leg to swell. He had to go in daily for radiation treatment and began to look very drawn and pale. During this period I hardly ever heard him utter a word of complaint. Soon Dad had received nine treatments of radiotherapy. He was so weak that he spent most of the day in bed. On the Saturday afternoon I went to see my parents and walked into the bedroom where Dad was lying down. He smiled as I walked in. His condition had deteriorated but there was an air of peacefulness about him.

"Dad, get better," I pleaded. I didn't stay long as Dad was too weak to sustain a conversation.

Little did I know that this would be the last time I would see my father alive. That evening Jeremy's friend rang our doorbell to say we must come at once to my mother's apartment as Dad had taken a bad turn. We had no telephone at the time, as we had just moved into our new apartment, and so they couldn't contact us any other way. I grabbed the car keys and Mervyn and I raced to my parents' apartment. As I pulled up outside I saw the ambulance speeding away down the road.

I kept praying silently: "Lord, please save Dad."

Mervyn and I rushed to Mom. Jeremy met me at the door. "What happened?" I queried. "Grandpa couldn't breathe," Jeremy said. "Granny called the doctor and he said it was serious. His pulse is very low." Mom related to me how Dad didn't want her to call a doctor. He said we have a doctor in the apartment, meaning 'Jeremy'. That was just like my father, intensely proud of his family even at such a time. I phoned the Casualty Section immediately, to find out what ward he had been put into.

The doctor was called to the telephone, Dad had died in the ambulance before arrival. Death was something we were not familiar with at home. Mom had lost most of her brothers and sisters but my children and I had never really experienced the death of someone so close to us. Still my mother was stunned. She never cried but just stared into space shaking her head in disbelief.

I could not sleep that night. I just tossed and turned and asked the Lord:

"Is Dad with you?" The Lord knew my heart and the following day he gave me the assurance that Dad was with Him. As we were all leaving to go to the funeral one of my cousins walked up to me.

"You really dishonoured your father by taking up the Christian faith, didn't you?" she said.

But during the funeral when the coffin was placed before us I felt the peace of the Lord within me and His words came to me:

I am the Resurrection and the Life. He that believeth in Me though he were dead, yet he shall live. John 11:25

While I was at the funeral my Pastor and the congregation were holding hands and praying for my father's healing, not knowing that he had already died. I was told that as they were praying, one of the ladies in the congregation had received a vision. She saw my father lying in a hospital bed. Coming towards him was an enormous light and my father rose up as Jesus held out his arms and embraced my father to take him home. When I heard of this vision I was at complete peace knowing that dad was with Jesus and that I would see him one day.

However, Mom took Dad's death very badly. She was heartbroken and she did not have the Lord in her life to support and console her. Together with other believers we interceded for her and the Lord gave me a vision. I saw my mother with her face lit up, the depressive expression had gone and there was a tree stump beside her. I held on to his vision for hope. Then, about six months later Mom too, became very ill. She lost consciousness one day and when she came round she was in a state of severe mental confusion. I was shocked to see her so deathly pale with her eyes and cheeks sunken in. While we were waiting for the doctor to arrive I began to pray for her. I spoke to her of how I loved her and how I told her that Dad was with the Lord, and if she wanted to see him again she would have to accept Jesus as her Messiah. I felt as if the Lord had broken her down and humbled her and that gradually she would realize who He really is and accept him as Messiah. Mom recovered in hospital, and my faith reassures me that her soul is in His safekeeping. Slowly the members of my family were coming to the Lord. I had prayed so much for them. Mom really needed me as she was 73 and could not walk too far.

I shuddered to think that only three years before the doctors had said that I would never walk again. I visited the neurosurgeon sometime after this to let him witness the miracle of my newly gained health. He nearly fell off his chair when he saw me walking into his consulting rooms spritely and erect and he rejoiced with me at my healing. He knew a miracle had taken place.

People who had witnessed me unable to walk, surrounded me for many months in amazement. I could do all the things a young healthy woman could do: walk, swim, run and carry things. Word of my miraculous healing spread everywhere, throughout my office building, my neighbourhood and beyond.

The testimony of my miraculous healing was published in the Christian Today magazine in South Africa. Soon I was being asked to give the testimony of my healing at churches and services all over Cape Town and thousands of people were reaping the fruits of my experience. Before my suffering I had taken so much for granted. I just thank the Lord for my miraculous healing. He has refined me through it all. To those who are searching for peace and fulfilment in their lives I say, look to the Lord Jesus Christ.

Jesus said: "*Peace I leave with you, my peace I give unto you: not as the world giveth, give I unto you." John 14:27*

He died for us so that we may have eternal life. And to the Jewish people, I say, you are God's chosen people. I pray that you will know the fulfilment and joy that I have found as a completed Jew. It is my prayer that you, too, will accept Jesus as your personal Saviour and Messiah and in so doing find the peace that I have found.

Isaiah 53:5 says: "He was wounded for our transgressions, He was bruised for our iniquities: the chastisement of our peace was upon Him: and with His stripes we are healed."

And by His Stripes, I have been miraculously healed.

The Lord calls His people to press on, to persevere, to pursue His desires with all diligence. For such He will do more than they can ever ask or imagine. Shalom and may you be encouraged and strengthened in your faith.

A Biblical Portrait of the Messiah found in both Covenants

by Rev. Alvin F. Showalter

SOURCE OF THE MESSIAH AND THE RESULTS OF HIS COMING

1. **Messiah, seed of woman, is victorious over the serpent (Satan):**

OLD COVENANT

"And I will put enmity between thee and the woman, and between thy seed and her seed: it shall bruise thy head, and thou shalt bruise his heel." Gen. 3:15 (See Isa. 7:14).

NEW COVENANT

"Forasmuch then as the children are partakers of flesh and blood, He (Christ) also Himself likewise took part of the same; that through death He might destroy him that had the power of death, that is, the devil." Heb. 2:14 (See Luke 1:26-38; John. 8:44, 12:30-33; Gal. 4:4-5; Col. 2:14-15; 1 John 3:8-10; Rev. 20:10, 12:5).

2. **Messiah is from the seed of Abraham, who is the father of many nations:**

OLD COVENANT

"Neither shall thy name any more be called Abram but thy name shall be Abraham; for a father of many nations have I made thee. And I will establish my covenant between me and thee and thy seed after thee in their generations for an everlasting covenant, to be a God unto thee, and to thy seed after thee." Gen. 17:5 (See Gen. 12:3, 18:18, 22:18).

NEW COVENANT

"For verily he took not on him the nature of angels; but he took on him the seed of Abraham." Heb. 2:16 (See Rom. 4:17).

"The book of the generation of Jesus Christ, the Son of David, the son of Abraham." Matt. 1:1 (See Gal. 3:16; Acts 3:25; Luke 3:34).

3. **Messiah is from the seed of Isaac:**

OLD COVENANT

"And God said unto Abraham, Let it not be grievous in thy sight because of the lad, and because of thy bondwoman; in all that Sarah hath said unto thee, hearken unto her voice; for in Isaac shall hy seed be called." Gen. 21:12 (See Gen. 17:19, 26:4).

NEW COVENANT

"By faith he sojourned in the land of promise, as in a strange country, dwelling in tabernacles with Isaac and Jacob, the heirs with him of the same promise: For he looked for a city which hath foundations, whose builder and maker is God." Heb. 11:9-10 (See Rom. 9:6-9; Heb. 11:18; Matt. 1:2; Luke 3:34).

4. **Messiah is from the seed of Jacob**:

OLD COVENANT

"I shall see him, but not now: I shall behold him, but not nigh: there shall come a Star out of Jacob, and a Sceptre shall rise out of Israel, and shall smite the corners of Moab, and destroy all the children of Sheth. - Out of Jacob shall come he that shall have dominion, and shall destroy him that remaineth of the city." Num. 24:17, 19 (See Gen. 28:4, 13-15).

NEW COVENANT

"By faith he sojourned in the land of promise, as in a strange country, dwelling in tabernacles with Isaac and Jacob, the heirs with him of the same promise: for he looked for a city which hath foundations, whose builder and maker is God." Heb. 11:9-10. "By faith Isaac blessed Jacob and Esau concerning things to come." Heb. 11:20 (See Acts 13:22-23; Rom. 9:9-13; Luke 3:34; Matt. 1:2).

5. **Messiah is from the seed of David:**

OLD COVENANT

"And there shall come forth a rod out of the stem of Jesse, and a Branch shall grow out of his roots." Isa. 11:1.

". . . I will set up thy seed after thee (David), which shall proceed out of thy bowels, and I will establish his kingdom . . . And thine house and thy kingdom shall be established for ever before thee: thy throne shall be established for ever." 2 Sam. 7:12b, 16 (See Isa. 9:7; Psa. 132:11).

NEW COVENANT

"Hath not the scripture said, That Christ cometh of the seed of David, and out of the town of Bethlehem, where David was?" John 7:42 (See Matt. 1:1, 6, 20; Acts 13:22-23).

"Which he had promised afore by his prophets in the holy scriptures, concerning his Son Jesus Christ our Lord, which was made of the seed of David according to the flesh." Rom. 1:2-3.

6. **Messiah shall sit on the throne of David, and rule over the house of Jacob:**

OLD COVENANT

"For unto us a child is born, unto us a son is given; and the government shall be upon his shoulder: and his name shall be called Wonderful, Councillor, The Mighty God, the Everlasting Father, the Prince of Peace. Of the increase of his government and peace there shall be no end, upon the throne of David, and upon his kingdom, to order it, and to establish it with judgment and with justice from henceforth even forever. The zeal of the Lord of hosts will perform this. The Lord sent a word into Jacob, and it hath lighted upon Israel." Isa. 9:6-8

NEW COVENANT

"He shall be great, and shall be called the Son of the Highest; and the Lord God shall give unto him the throne of his father David: And he shall reign over the house of Jacob for ever; and of his kingdom there shall be no end." Luke 1:32 (See Acts 3:25-26; 13:22-23).

7. **Messiah (Shiloh) is from the tribe of Judah:**

OLD COVENANT

"The Sceptre shall not depart from Judah, nor a lawgiver from between his feet, until SHILOH come; and unto him shall the gathering of the people be." Gen. 49:10 (See Dan. 9:25). Sceptre (Rulership) Micah 5:1-2; Num. 24:17 SHILOH means either "the Sent One," :the Peace-bringer," or "He whose right it is."

NEW COVENANT

"For it is evident that our Lord sprang out of Judah; of which tribe Moses spake nothing concerning priesthood." Heb. 7:14. "But unto the Son he saith, Thy throne, O God, is for ever and ever: a sceptre of righteousness is the sceptre of thy kingdom." Heb. 1:8 (See Psa. 45:6; Rev. 5:5; Matt. 1:2-3; Luke 2:1-6, 3:33).

8. **Messiah is from Israel, like unto Moses, and speaks God's words:**

OLD COVENANT

"The Lord thy God will raise up unto thee a Prophet from the midst of thee, of thy brethren, like unto me; unto him ye shall hearken . . . I will raise them up, a Prophet from among their brethren, like unto thee, and will put my words in his mouth; and he shall speak unto them all that I shall command him. And it shall come to pass, that whosoever will not hearken unto my words which he shall speak in my name, I will require it of him." Deut. 18:15, 18-19.

NEW COVENANT

"This is that Moses, which said unto the children of Israel, A prophet shall the Lord your God raise up unto you of your brethren like unto me; him shall ye hear." Acts 7:37 (See John 6:14, 7:40; Acts 3:19-25; Heb. 2:17). "For I have not spoken of myself; but the Father which sent me, he gave me a commandment, what I should say, and what I should speak." John 12:49 (See John 12:48).

9. **Messiah is set for the fall and the rising again of Israel:**

OLD COVENANT

"Sanctify the Lord of hosts himself; and let him be your fear, and let him be your dread. And he shall be for a sanctuary, but for a stone of stumbling and for a rock of offence to both the houses of Israel, for a gin (trap) and for a snare to the inhabitants of Jerusalem. And many among them shall stumble, and fall, and be broken, and be snared, and be taken." Isa. 8:1315 (See Micah 5:3; Hosea 5:14-15).

NEW COVENANT

"And Simeon blessed them and said unto Mary his mother, Behold, this child is set for the fall and rising again of many in Israel; and for a sign which shall be spoken against; Yea, a sword shall pierce through thy own soul also, that the thoughts of many hearts may be revealed." Luke 2:34-35 (See Acts 3:13-26).

EVIDENCE THAT THE MESSIAH HAS COME

10. **Messiah was born in Bethlehem:**

OLD COVENANT

"But thou, Bethlehem Ephratah, though thou be little among the thousands of Judah, yet out of thee shall be come forth unto me that is to be ruler in Israel; whose goings forth have been from of old, from everlasting. Therefore will he give them up, until time that she which travaileth hath brough forth; then the remnant of his brethren shall return unto the children of Israel." Micah 5:2-3.

NEW COVENANT

"Hath not the scripture said, That Christ cometh of the seed of David, and out of the town of Bethlehem, where David was? John 7:42 (See Matt. 2:56; Luke 2:4-6, 11). "Now when Jesus was born in Bethlehem of Judea in the days of Herod the King, behold, there came wise men from the east to Jerusalem." Matt. 2:1.

11. **Messiah was born of a virgin:**

OLD COVENANT

"Therefore the Lord himself shall give you a sign; Behold, a virgin shall conceive, and bear a son, and shall call his name Immanuel." Isa. 7:14 (See Gen. 3:15; Isa. 9:6; Jer. 31:22; Psa. 2:7).

NEW COVENANT

"And the angel answered and said unto her, The Holy Ghost shall come upon thee, and the power of the Highest shall overshadow thee; therefore also that holy thing which shall be born of thee shall be called the Son of God." Luke 1:35 (See Matt. 1:18, 22-23; Luke 1:26-35; 2:7).

12. **Messiah was called out of Egypt:**

OLD COVENANT

"When Israel was a child, then I loved him, and called my son out of Egypt." Hosea 11:1 (See Hosea 13:4; Ex. 4:22).

NEW COVENANT

"And was there until the death of Herod: that it might be fulfilled which was spoken of the Lord by the prophet, saying, Out of Egypt have I called my son." Matt. 2:15 (See Matt. 2:14).

13. **Messenger prepared the way for the Messiah at His First Coming, to suffer:**

OLD COVENANT

"Behold, I will send my messenger, and he shall prepare the way before me; and the Lord, whom ye seek, shall suddenly come to his temple, even the messenger of the covenant, whom ye delight in: behold, he shall come, saith the Lord of hosts." Mal. 3:1 (See Mal. 4:5; Matt. 11:14).

NEW COVENANT

". . . Jesus began to say unto the multitudes concerning John. For this is he, of whom it is written, Behold, I send my messenger before thy face, which shall prepare thy way before thee." Matt. 11:7b, 10 (See Matt. 11:11-14; Luke 1:76-79; John 1:6-7, 19-23).

14. **Messiah was a light in Galilee of the nations:**

OLD COVENANT

"Nevertheless the dimness shall not be such as was in her vexation, when at first he lightly afflicted the land of Zebulun and the land of Naphtali, and afterward did more grievously afflict her by the way of the sea, beyond Jordan in Galilee of the nations. The people that walked in darkness have seen a great light: they that dwell in the land of the shadow of death, upon them hath the light shined." Isa. 9:1-2 (See Isa. 60: 1-3, 19; Micah 7:8-9).

NEW COVENANT

"And leaving Nazareth, he came and dwelt in Capernaum, which is upon the sea coast, in the borders of Zebulun and Naphtali: that it might be fulfilled which was spoken by Isaiah the prophet, saying, The land of Zebulun, and the land of Naphtali, by the way of the sea beyond Jordan. Galilee of the Gentiles; the people which sat in darkness saw great light; and to them which sat in the region and shadow of death light is sprung up." Matt. 4:1316 (See Luke 1:76-80; 2:32; John 8:12; 12:35-36, 46; Eph. 5:8, 13-14; 1 Pet. 2:9 1 John 1:5, 7).

15. **Messiah spoke in parables:**

OLD COVENANT

"I will open my mouth in a parable: I will utter dark sayings of old: which we have heard and known, and our fathers have told us." Psa. 78:2-3 (See Psa. 49:4; Prov. 1:5-6).

NEW COVENANT

"All these things spake Jesus unto the multitude in parables; and without a parable spake he not unto them: that it might be fulfilled which was spoken by the prophet, saying, I will open my mouth in parables, I will utter things which have been kept secret from the foundation of the world." Matt. 13:34-35 (See Matt. 13:13-15; Mark 4:33-34).

16. **Messiah rode in Jerusalem on an ass:**

OLD COVENANT

"Rejoice greatly, O daughter of Zion; shout, O daughter of Jerusalem: behold, the King cometh unto thee: he is just, and having salvation; lowly, and riding upon an ass, and upon a colt the foal of an ass." Zech. 9:9 (See Isa. 62:11).

NEW COVENANT

"And Jesus, when he had found a young ass, sat thereon; as it is written, Fear not, daughter of Zion: behold thy King cometh, sitting on an ass's colt." John 12:14-15 (See Matt. 21:4-7; Mark 11:7-10; Luke 19:35-39; John 12:12-15).

17. **They said concerning the Messiah,"Blessed be He that cometh in the name of the Lord":**

OLD COVENANT

"Save now, I beseech thee, O Lord: O Lord, I beseech thee, send now prosperity. Blessed be he that cometh in the name of the Lord: we have blessed you out of the house of the Lord." Psa. 118:25-26 (See Psa. 72:17-19).

NEW COVENANT

"On the next day much people that were come to the feast, when they heard that Jesus was coming to Jerusalem, took branches of palm trees, and went forth to meet him, and cried, Hosanna: Blessed is the King of Israel that cometh in the name of the Lord." John 12:12-13 (See Mark 11:8-10; Matt. 21:8-9; Luke 19:35-38).

18. **Messiah was sold for thirty pieces of silver:**

OLD COVENANT

"And I said unto them, if ye think good give me my price: and if not, forbear. So they weighed for my price thirty pieces of silver. And the Lord said unto me, cast it unto the potter: a goodly price that I was prized at of them. And I took the thirty pieces of silver, and cast them to the potter in the house of the Lord." Zech. 11:12-13 (See Psa. 41:9; 69:25-28).

NEW COVENANT

"Then one of the twelve, called Judas Iscariot, went unto the chief priests, and said unto them, What will ye give me, and I will deliver him unto you? And they covenanted with him for thirty pieces of silver. And from that time he sought opportunity to betray him." Matt. 26:14-16 (See Matt. 27:3, 9-10; Acts 1:16-20).

19. **Messiah was betrayed:**

OLD COVENANT

"Yea, mine own familiar friend, in whom I trusted, which did eat of my bread, hath lifted up his heel against me." Psa. 41:9 (See Psa. 55:12-15; 69:25; 109:8).

NEW COVENANT

"And supper being ended, the devil having now put into the heart of Judas Iscariot, Simon's son, to betray him: . . . I speak not of you all: I know whom I have chosen: but that the Scripture may be fulfilled, He that eateth bread with me hath lifted up his heel against me. Now I tell you before it come, that, when it is come to pass, ye may believe that I am he." John 13:2, 18-19 (See Matt. 26:23-25; 27:3-5; Mark 14:18; Acts 1:20).

20. **Messiah was hated without a cause:**

OLD COVENANT

"They that hate me without a cause are more than the hairs of mine head: they that would destroy me, being mine enemies wrongfully, are mighty: then I restored that which I took not away." Psa. 69:4 (See Psa. 109:2-5; 35:19; 7:4; Isa. 49:7).

NEW COVENANT

"If I had not done among them the works which none other man did, they had not had sin: But now have they both seen and hated both me and my Father. But this cometh to pass, that the word might be fulfilled that is written in their law. They hated me without a cause. " John 15:24-25.

21. **Messiah spoke not a word before his accusers:**

OLD COVENANT

"He was oppressed, and he was afflicted, yet he opened not his mouth: He is brought as a lamb to the slaughter, and as a sheep before her shearers is dumb, so he openeth not his mouth." Isa. 53:7 (See Isa. 42:2; Psa. 38:13-14).

NEW COVENANT

"Then he questioned with him in many words; but he answered him nothing." Luke 23:9 (See Matt. 27:12; Mark 15:3-5; Acts 8:32-35; Matt. 26:62-63; Matt. 12:15-19).

22. **Messiah suffered:**

OLD COVENANT

"Surely he hath borne our griefs, and carried our sorrows: yet we did esteem him stricken, smitten of God, and afflicted." Isa. 53:4 (See Psa. 22).

NEW COVENANT

"But those things, which God before had showed by the mouth of all his prophets, that Christ should suffer, he hath so fulfilled." Acts 3:18 (See Acts 17:2-3; 26:22-23; Luke 24:25-27; 1 Pet. 1:10-11).

23. **Messiah was spate upon:**

OLD COVENANT

"I gave my back to the smiters, and my cheeks to them that plucked off the hair: I hid not my face from shame and spitting." Isa. 50:6 (See Psa. 22:7-8).

NEW COVENANT

"Then did they spit in his face, and buffeted him: and others smote him with the palms of their hands, saying, Prophesy unto us, thou Christ, who is he that smote thee?" Matt. 26:67-68 (See Mark 14:65; 15:19; John 18:22; 19:1-3).

24. **Messiah was mocked and spitefully entreated:**

OLD COVENANT

"As many were astonished at thee; his visage was so marred more than any man, and his form more than the sons of men." Isa. 52:14. "I gave my back to the smiters, and my cheeks to them that plucked off the hair: I hid not my face from shame and spitting." Isa. 50:6 (See Psa. 35:1516; 22:7-8).

NEW COVENANT

"For he shall be delivered unto the Gentiles, and shall be mocked, and spitefully entreated, and spitted on: And they shall scourge him, and put him to death: And the third day he shall rise again." Luke 18:32-33 (See Matt. 27:27-44; Luke 23:10-11; Mark 15:29-32).

25. **Messiah was scourged:**

OLD COVENANT

"But he was wounded for our transgressions, he was bruised for our iniquities: the chastisement of our peace was upon him; and with his stripes we are healed." Isa. 53:5 (See Psa. 22:7-8; Isa 50:6; Micah 5:1; Isa. 52:14; 53:3).

NEW COVENANT

"Then Pilate therefore took Jesus, and scourged him. And the solders plaited a crown of thorns, and put it on his head, and they put on him a purple robe, and said, Hail, King of the Jews! and they smote him with their hands." John 19:1-3 (See Matt. 8:16-17; 27:27-30; Mark 14:65).

26. **Messiah was given vinegar to drink:**

OLD COVENANT

"They gave me also gall for my meat; and in my thirst they gave me vinegar to drink." Psa. 69:21.

NEW COVENANT

"And the soldiers also mocked him, coming to him, and offering him vinegar." Luke 23:36 (See Matt. 27:34, 48; Mark 15:36; John 19:28-30).

27. **Messiah's garments were parted by lots:**

OLD COVENANT

"They part my garments among them and cast lots upon my vesture." Psa. 22:18.

NEW COVENANT

"Then said Jesus, Father, forgive them: for they know not what they do. And they parted his raiment, and cast lots." Luke 23:34 (See Matt. 27:35; Mark 15:24; John 19:23-24).

28. **Messiah thirsted:**

OLD COVENANT

"My strength is dried up like a potsherd: and my tongue cleaveth to my jaws: and thou hast brought me into the dust of death." Psa. 22:15 (See Psa. 69:21).

NEW COVENANT

"After this, Jesus knowing that all things were now accomplished, that the scripture might be fulfilled, saith, I thirst." John 19:28 (See Matt. 27:48).

29. **Messiah's hands and feet were pierced:**

OLD COVENANT

"For dogs have compassed me: the assembly of the wicked have enclosed me: they pierced my hands and my feet." Psa. 22:16 (See Zech. 12:10; 13:6).

NEW COVENANT

"Then saith he to Thomas, reach hither thy finger, and behold my hands; and reach hither thy hand, and thrust it into my side: and be not faithless, but believing. And Thomas answered and said unto him, My Lord and My God." John 20:27-28 (See Matt. 27:35a; Luke 23:33; John 19:34, 37; 20:25).

30. **Israel will look upon the Messiah whom they have pierced:**

OLD COVENANT

"And I will pour upon the house of David, and upon the inhabitants of Jerusalem, the spirit of grace and of supplication: and they shall look upon me whom they have pierced, and they shall mourn for him, as one mourneth for his only son, and shall be in bitterness for him, as one that is in bitterness for his first-born." Zech. 12:10

NEW COVENANT

"But one of the soldiers with a spear pierced his side, and forthwith came there out blood and water . . . For these things were done, that the scripture should be fulfilled . . . They shall look on him whom they pierced." John 19:34, 36a, 37b (See Luke 2:35; Rev 1:7). (This happened some 2 000 years ago and will also happen with great bitterness at His final coming.)

31. **Messiah prayed for his enemies:**

OLD COVENANT

"Therefore will I divide him a portion with the great, and he shall divide the spoil with the strong; because he hath poured out his soul unto death: and he was numbered with the transgressors; and bare the sin of many, and made intercession for the transgressors." Isa. 53:12 (See Psa. 109:4).

NEW COVENANT

"Then said Jesus, Father, forgive them; for they know not what they do. And they parted his raiment, and cast lots." Luke 23:34.

32. **Messiah said, "My God, why hast thou forsaken me?":**

OLD COVENANT

"My God, my God, why hast thou forsaken me? Why art thou so far from helping me, and from the words of my roaring?" Psa. 22:1.

NEW COVENANT

"And about the ninth hour Jesus cried with a loud voice, saying, Eli, Eli, lama sabachthani? That is to say, My God, my God, why have you forsaken me?" Matt. 27:46 (See Mark 15:34).

33. **Messiah died with the malefactors:**

OLD COVENANT

"Therefore will I divide him a portion with the great, and he shall divide the spoil with the strong; because he hath poured out his soul unto death; and he was numbered with the transgressors; and he bare the sin of many, and made intercession for the transgressors." Isa. 53:12.

NEW COVENANT

"Where they crucified him, and two others with him, on either side one, and Jesus in the midst. And Pilate wrote a tile, and put in on the cross. And the writing was JESUS OF NAZARETH THE KING OF THE JEWS." John 19:18-19 (See Matt. 27:38; Mark 15:27-28; Luke 23:33).

34. **Messiah was in the grave three days and three nights:**

OLD COVENANT

"Now the Lord had prepared a great fish to swallow up Jonah. And Jonah was in the belly of the fish three days and three nights." Jonah 1:17 (See Hosea 6:1-3; Jonah 2:1-10).

NEW COVENANT

"But he answered and said unto them, An evil and adulterous generation seeketh after a sign; and there shall no sign be given to it, but the sign of the prophet Jonah: for as Jonah was three days and three nights in the whale's belly; so shall the Son of man be three days and three nights in the heart of the earth." Matt. 12:39-40 (See Luke 11:29-30).

35. **Messiah was buried in a rich man's tomb:**

OLD COVENANT

"And he made his grave with the wicked, and with the rich in his death; because he had done no violence. neither was any deceit in his mouth." Isa. 53:9

NEW COVENANT

"And when Joseph (rich man) had taken the body, he wrapped it in a clean linen cloth, and laid it in his own new tomb, which he had hewn out in the rock: and he rolled a great stone to the door of the sepulcher, and departed." Matt. 27:59-60.

36. **Messiah was the crucified One:**

OLD COVENANT

"My God, my God, why hast thou forsaken me? . . . I am poured out like water, and all my bones are out of joint: my heart is like wax; it is melted in the midst of my bowels . . . For dogs have compassed me: the assembly of the wicked have enclosed me: they pierced my hands and my feet. I may tell all my bones: they look and stare upon me. They part my garments among them, and cast lots upon my vesture." Psa. 22:1a, 14, 16-18 (See Isa. 53: 5-12).

NEW COVENANT

"Therefore let all the house of Israel know assuredly, that God hath made that same Jesus, whom ye have crucified, both Lord and Christ." Acts 2:36 "And when they had mocked him, they took off the purple from him, and put his own clothes on him, and led him out to crucify him . . . And when they had crucified him, they parted his garments, casting lots upon them, what every man should take. And it was the third hour, and they crucified him." Mark 15:20, 24-25 (See Matt. 27:31; John 1:29; 19:15-18; 20:25-27; 1 Cor. 15:3).

37. **Messiah was rejected -"Who hath believed our report?":**

OLD COVENANT

"Who hath believed our report? And to whom is the arm of the Lord revealed? . . . He is despised and rejected of men; a man of sorrows, and acquainted with grief: and we hid as it were our faces from him; he was despised, and we esteemed him not." Isa. 53:1, 3 (See Psa. 2:2; 69:8).

NEW COVENANT

"But though he had done so many miracles before them, yet they believed not on him: that saying of Isaiah the prophet might be fulfilled, which he spake, Lord, who hath believed our report? And to whom hath the arm of the Lord been revealed?" John 12:37-38 (See john 1:11-12; 5:43; Acts 4:26-28; Luke 4:29; 17:25; 23:18).

REASON AND NEED FOR THE MESSIAH'S COMING

38. **Messiah is a sign to Israel:**

OLD COVENANT

"Behold, I and the children whom the Lord hath given me are for signs and for wonders in Israel from the Lord of hosts, which dwelleth in mount Zion." Isa. 8:18 (See Heb. 2:13; Isa. 7:14).

NEW COVENANT

"And Simeon blessed them, and said unto Mary his mother, Behold, this child is set for the fall and rising again of many in Israel; and for a sign which shall be spoken against." Luke 2:34 (See Matt. 12:39-40; 1 Cor 1:22).

39. **Messiah's atonement needed by Jews and Gentiles, because all have sinned:**

OLD COVENANT

"Ah sinful nation, a people laden with iniquity, a seed of evildoers, children that are corrupters: they have forsaken the Lord, they have provoked the Holy One of Israel unto anger, they are gone away backward." Isa. 1:4. "All we like sheep have gone astray; we have turned everyone to his own way; and the Lord hath laid on him the iniquity of us all." Isa. 53:6.

NEW COVENANT

"What then? Are we better than they? No, in no wise: for we have before proved both Jews and Gentiles, that they are all under sin; As it is written, There is none righteous, no not one." Rom. 3:9-10. "For He (God) hath made him (Christ) to be sin for us, who knew no sin; that we might be made the righteousness of God in him." 2 Cor. 5:21 (See Rom. 11:32).

40. **Messiah must die for the atonement of His people's sins:**

OLD COVENANT

"He was taken from prison and from judgment: and who shall declare his generation? For he was cut off out of the land of the living: for the transgression of my people was he stricken." Isa. 53:8. "Yet it pleased the Lord to bruise him: he hath put him to grief: when thou shalt make his soul an offering for sin, he shall see his seed, he shall prolong his days, and the pleasure of the Lord shall prosper in his hand." Isa. 53:10 (See Dan. 9:26; Isa. 53:12).

NEW COVENANT

“And one of them, named Caiaphas, being the high priest that same year, said unto them, Ye know nothing at all, nor consider that it is expedient for us, that one man should die for the people, and that the whole nation perish not. And this spake he not of himself: but being high priest that year, he prophesied that Jesus should die for that nation; And not for that nation only, but that also he should gather together in one the children of God that were scattered abroad.” John 11:49-52 (See Matt. 27:50-54).

41. **Messiah bore out infirmities:**

OLD COVENANT

“Surely he hath borne our griefs, and carried our sorrows; yet we did esteem him stricken, smitten of God, and afflicted. But he was wounded for our transgressions, he was bruised for our iniquities: the chastisement of our peace was upon him; and with his stripes we are healed.” Isa. 53:4-5 (See Isa. 35:5-6; 40:11; 42:3).

NEW COVENANT

“When the even was come, they brought unto him many that were possessed with devils: and he cast out the spirits with his word, and healed all that were sick: That it might be fulfilled which was spoken by Isaiah the prophet, saying, Himself took our infirmities, and bare our sicknesses.” Matt. 8:16-17 (See Heb. 4:15; Matt. 11:4-5; 12:15, 20).

42. **Messiah bore our sins:**

OLD COVENANT

“. . . and he bare the sin of many, and made intercession for the transgressors.” Isa. 53:12b (See Dan. 9:24-26; Psa 22:6; 69:7; 9:20 Isa. 53:4-6)

NEW COVENANT

“For he hath made him to be sin for us, who knew no sin; that we might be made the righteousness of God in him.” 2 Cor 5:21 (See Rom. 15:3; Matt. 20:28).

43. **Messiah will save those from sin who believe in Him:**

OLD COVENANT

“I will declare the decree: the Lord hath said unto me, Thou art my Son; this day have I begotten thee . . . Kiss the Son, lest he be angry, and ye perish from the way, when his wrath is kindled but a little. Blessed are all they that put their trust in him.” Psa. 2:7, 12 (See Isa. 43:10-13; 45:22).

NEW COVENANT

"And many other signs truly did Jesus in the presence of his disciples, which are not written in this book: but these are written, that ye might believe that Jesus is the Christ, the Son of God; and that believing ye might have life through his name." John 20:30-31.

44. **Messiah gives individual peace:**

OLD COVENANT

"The Lord lift up his countenance upon thee, and give thee peace." Num. 6:26. "The Lord will give strength unto his people; the Lord will bless his people with peace." Psa. 29:11. "Thou wilt keep him in perfect peace, whose mind is stayed on thee: because he trusteth in thee." Isa. 26:3 (See Isa. 9:6-7; 53:5).

NEW COVENANT

"Peace I leave with you, my peace I give unto you: not as the world giveth, give I unto you. Let not your heart be troubled neither let it be afraid." John 14:27. "These things I have spoken unto you, that in me might have peace. In the world ye shall have tribulation: but be of good cheer; I have overcome the world." John 16:33 (See Rom. 5:1; 2 Thess. 3:16).

45. **Messiah gives resurrection life:**

OLD COVENANT

"And many of them that sleep in the dust of the earth shall awake, some to everlasting life, and some to shame and everlasting contempt." Dan. 12:2 (See Job 19:26; Psa. 17:15).

NEW COVENANT

"Verily, verily, I say unto you, The hour is coming, and now is, when the dead shall hear the voice of the Son of God: and they that hear shall live . . . And shall come forth; they that have done good, unto the resurrection of life; and they that have done evil, unto the resurrection of damnation." John 5:25, 29.

CHARACTER OF THE MESSIAH

46. Messiah is our shepherd:

OLD COVENANT

"He shall feed his flock like a shepherd: he shall gather the lambs with his arm, and carry them in his bosom, and shall gently lead those that are with young." Isa.

40:11 (See Ezek. 34:23).

NEW COVENANT

"I am the good shepherd: the good shepherd giveth his life for the sheep." John 10:11 (See Heb. 13:20).

47. **Messiah's bones not broken, as the Passover Lamb:**

OLD COVENANT

"They shall leave none of it unto the morning, nor break any bone of it: according to all the ordinances of the Passover they shall keep it." Num. 9:12 (See Ex. 12:46; Psa. 22:17; 34:20).

NEW COVENANT

"Then came the soldiers, and brake the legs of the first, and the other which was crucified with him. But when they came to Jesus, and saw that he was dead already, they break not his legs . . . For these things were done, that the scripture should be fulfilled, A bone of him shall not be broken." John 19:32-33, 36.

48. **Messiah is our Passover Lamb:**

OLD COVENANT

"Then Moses called for all the elders of Israel, and said unto them, Draw out and take you a lamb according to your families, and kill the Passover. And ye shall take a bunch of hyssop, and dip it in the blood that is in the basin, and strike the lintel and the two side posts with the blood that is in the basin; and none of you shall go out at the door of his house until the morning." Ex. 12:21-22 (See Isa. 53:7).

NEW COVENANT

"Purge out therefore the old leaven, that ye may be a new lump, as ye are unleavened. For even Christ our Passover is sacrificed for us. Therefore let us keep the feast, not with old leaven, neither with the leaven of malice and wickedness; but with the unleavened bread of sincerity and truth." 1 Cor. 5:7-8. "The next day John seeth Jesus coming unto him, and saith, Behold the Lamb of God, which taketh away the sin of the world." John 1:29

REACTION OF ISRAEL AND THE GENTILES TO THE MESSIAH

49. **Messiah was not understood by His people:**

OLD COVENANT

"And he said, Go and tell this people, Hear ye indeed, but understand not; and see ye indeed, but perceive not." Isa. 6:9.

NEW COVENANT

"Therefore speak I to them in parables: because they seeing see not; and hearing they hear not, neither do they understand. And in them is fulfilled the prophecy of Isaiah, which saith, By hearing ye shall hear, and shall not understand; and seeing ye shall see, and shall not perceive." Matt. 13:1314 (See Matt. 13:15-17).

50. **Israel has blinded eyes and hardened hearts towards the Messiah:**

OLD COVENANT

"And he said, Go, and tell this people, Hear ye indeed, but understand not; and see ye indeed, but perceive not. Make the heart of this people fat, and make their ears heavy, and shut their eyes; lest they see with their eyes, and hear with their ears, and understand with their heart, and convert, and be healed." Isa. 6:9-10 (See Isa. 29:13-14; Jer. 5:20-23; Psa. 69:22).

NEW COVENANT

"But though he had done so many miracles befoe them, yet they believed, not on him . . . Therefore they could not believe because that Isaiah said again, He hath blinded their eyes, and hardened their heart; that they should not see with their eyes, nor understand with their heart, and be converted, and I should heal them. These things said Isaiah, when he saw his glory, and spake of him." John 12:37, 39-41 (See Matt. 13: 14-17; Acts 28: 24-27; Rom. 11:8-9).

51. **Messiah, shepherd, was smitten and His flock was scattered; eventually regathered to Israel:**

OLD COVENANT

"Awake, O sword, against my shepherd and against the man that is my fellow, saith the Lord of hosts: smite the shepherd, and the sheep shall be scattered: and I will turn mine hand upon the little ones." Zech. 13:7 "And the Lord shall scatter you among the nations, and ye shall be left few in number among the heathen, whither the Lord shall lead you." Deut. 4:27 (See Deut. 28:64a; Lev. 26:33 Ezek. 11:17; 34:5-6; Jer. 16:14-15; 23:3).

NEW COVENANT

"Then saith Jesus unto them, All ye shall be offended because of me this night; for it is written, I will smite the shepherd, and the sheep of the flock shall be scattered abroad." Matt. 26:31. "Jeus answered them. Do ye now believe? Behold, the hour cometh, yea, is now come, that ye shall be scattered, every man to his own, and shall leave me alone: and yet I am not alone, because the Father is with me." John 16:31-32 (See Rom. 11:15, 23, 25-26; John 11:51-52; Luke 2:34).

52. **Messiah, a stone set at naught, will be a cornerstone:**

OLD COVENANT

"The stone which the builders refused is become the head stone of the corner." Psa. 118:22. "Sanctify the Lord of hosts himself; and let him be your fear, and let him be your dread. And he shall be for a sanctuary; but for a stone of stumbling and for a rock of offense to both the houses of Israel, for a gin and for a snare to the inhabitants of Jerusalem." Isa. 8:13-14. "Therefore thus saith the Lord God, Behold, I lay in Zion for a foundation a stone, a tried stone, a precious corner stone, a sure foundation: he that believeth shall not make haste," Isa 28:16.

NEW COVENANT

"Be it known unto you all, and to all the people of Israel, that by the name of Jesus Christ of Nazareth, whom ye crucified, whom God raised from the dead, even by him doth this man stand here before you whole. This is the

stone which was set at naught of you builders, which is become the head of the corner. Neither is there salvation in any other: for there is none other name under heaven given among men whereby we must be saved." Acts 4:10-12. ". . . for they drank of that spiritual Rock that followed them: and that Rock was Christ." 1 Cor. 10:4b (See Matt. 21:42, 44; Mark 12:10-11; Rom. 9:32-33; 1 Pet. 2:6-8).

53. **Messiah was received by the Gentiles:**

OLD COVENANT

"And I will bless them that bless thee, and curse him that curseth thee: and in thee shall all families of the earth be blessed." Gen. 12:3. "And I will sow her unto me in the earth; and I will have mercy upon her that had not obtained mercy; and I will say to them which were not my people, thou are my people and they shall say, Thou art my God." Hosea 2:23 (See Isa. 49:6; Mal. 1:11; Deut. 32:21; Isa. 65:1 Isa. 11:10; 42:1)

NEW COVENANT

"And the scripture, foreseeing that God would justify the heathen through faith, preached before the gospel unto Abraham, saying, in thee shall all nations be blessed." Gal. 3:8. "Even us, whom he hath called, not of the Jews only, but also of the Gentiles? As he saith also in Hosea, I will call them my people, which were not my people; and her beloved, which was not beloved." Rom. 9:24-25 (See Acts 13: 46-47; Rom. 10:18, 21; John 10:16; Acts 10:45, 47).

MESSIAH'S PRESENT POSITION

54. **Messiah was resurrected and lives today:**

OLD COVENANT

"For thou will not leave my soul in hell; neither wilt thou suffer thine Holy One to see corruption." Psa. 16:10 (See Psa. 16:11). "None of them can by any means redeem his brother, nor give to God a ransom for him; (for the redemption of their soul is precious, and it ceaseth for ever:) that he should still live for ever, and not see corruption." Psa. 49:7-9 (See Job 19:25-27; Psa. 71:20; Isa. 26:19; Hosea 6:1-2).

NEW COVENANT

"Be it know unto you all, and to all the people of Israel, that by the name of Jesus Christ of Nazareth, whom ye crucified, whom God raised from the dead, even by him doth this man stand here before you whole." Acts 4:10 (See Matt. 16:21; 28:5-6; Luke 18:33; John 13:36 Acts 2:24-28, 30-32; 13:30; Rom. 1:3-4; Heb. 7:25; Luke 24:6, 31, 34-40).

55. **Messiah has ascended into heaven:**

OLD COVENANT

"Thou has ascended on high, thou has led captivity captive: thou hast received gifts for men: yea, for the rebellious also, that the Lord God might dwell among them. Blessed be the Lord, who daily loadeth us with benefits, even the God of our salvation. Selah." Psa. 68:18-19 (See Psa. 16: 10-11).

NEW COVENANT

"Wherefore he saith, When he ascended up on high, he led captivity captive, and gave gifts unto men. Now that he ascended, what is it but that he also descended first into the lower parts of the earth? He that descended is the same also that ascended up far above all heavens, that he might fill all things." Eph. 4:8-10 (See John 20: 16-17; Acts 1:9-11 1 Peter 3:18-22; Luke 24:50-51).

56. **Messiah is on the right hand of God:**

OLD COVENANT

"The Lord said unto my Lord, Sit thou at my right hand, until I make thine enemies thy footstool." Psa. 110:1. "For thou will not leave my soul in hell; neither wilt thou suffer thine Holy One to see corruption. Thou wilt show me the path of life; in thy presence is fullness of joy; at thy right hand there are pleasures for evermore." Psa. 16:10-11 (See Psa. 68:18; 80:17; Hosea 5:15).

NEW COVENANT

" And Jesus said, I am; and ye shall see the Son of man sitting on the right hand of power, and coming in the clouds of heaven." Mark 14:62. "The God of our fathers raised up Jesus, whom ye slew and hanged on a tree, Him hath God exalted with his right hand to be a Prince and a Saviour, for to give repentance to Israel, and forgiveness of sins." Acts 5:30-31 (See Mat. 26:64; Mark 13:26; Acts 2:34-36; Heb. 1:3; 10:12-13).

MESSIAH'S FUTURE COMING

57. **Messiah has not forsaken Israel:**

OLD COVENANT

"If those ordinances depart from before me, saith the Lord, then the seed of Israel also shall cease from being a nation before me forever. Thus saith the Lord; if heaven above can be measured, and the foundations of the earth searched out beneath, I will also cast off all the seed of Israel for all that they have done saith the Lord." Jer. 31:36-37 (See Gen. 8:21-22; Jer. 33:20-21, 25-

26). NEW COVENANT

"I say then, Hath God cast away his people? God forbid. For I also am an Israelite, of the seed of Abraham, of the tribe of Benjamin. God hath not cast away his people which he foreknew . . . Even so then at this present time also there is a remnant according to the election of grace." Rom. 11:12a, 5 (See Rom. 11:25-27).

58. **"The time of Jacob's trouble" will lead to Israel's national repentance and the appearance of the pierced Messiah:**

OLD COVENANT

"Ask ye now, and see whether a man doth travail with child? Wherefore do I see every man with his hands on his loins, as a woman in travail, and all faces are turned into paleness? Alas! For that day is great so that none is like it: It is even the time of Jacob's trouble; but he shall be saved out of it." Jer. 30:6-7. "And I will pour upon the house of David, and upon the inhabitants of Jerusalem, the spirit of grace and of supplication: and they shall look upon me whom they have pierced, and they shall mourn for him, as one mourneth for his only son, and shall be in bitterness for him, as one that is in bitterness for his firstborn." Zech. 12:10 (See Zech. 12:2-3, 11-14).

NEW COVENANT

"Behold, he cometh with clouds; and every eye shall see him, and they also which pierced him: and all kindreds of the earth shall wail because of him, Even so, Amen, I am Alpha and Omega, the beginning and the ending, saith the Lord, which is, and which was, and which is to come, the Almighty. I, John, who also am your brother, and companion in tribulation, and in the kingdom and patience of Jesus Christ, was in the isle that is called Patmos, for the word of God, and for the testimony of Jesus Christ." Rev. 1:7-9 (See Matt. 24:29-31; Mark 13:14-27; Luke 21:20-28).

59. **Messengers will prepare the way for the Messiah at His second coming, to reign:**

OLD COVENANT

"And two olive trees by it, one upon the right side of the bowl, and the other upon the left side thereof . . . Then said he, These are the two anointed ones, and that stand by the Lord of the whole earth." Zech. 4:3, 14. "Behold, I will send you Elijah the prophet before the coming of the great and dreadful day of the Lord." Mal. 4:5 (See Isa. 40:1-3; Psa. 2:6).

NEW COVENANT

"And I will give power unto my two witnesses, and they shall prophesy a thousand two hundred and three-score days, clothed in sackcloth. These are two olive trees, and the two candlesticks standing before the God of the earth." Rev. 11:3-4. (These two may be Moses and Elijah as a last testimony of the law and prophets before the final reign of the Messiah.)

60. **Messiah will come again and will stand on the Mount of Olives:**

OLD COVENANT

"Then shall the Lord go forth, and fight against those nations, as when he fought in the day of battle. And his feet shall stand in that day upon the mount of Olives, which is before Jerusalem on the east, and the mount of Olives shall cleave in the midst thereof towards the east and towards the west, and there shall be a very great valley; and half of the mountain shall remove toward the north, and half of it toward the south." Zech. 14:3-4 (See Dan. 7:13-14).

NEW COVENANT

"And while they looked steadfastly towards heaven as he went up, behold, to men stood by them in white apparel; Which also said, Ye men of Galilee, why stand ye gazing up into heaven? This same Jesus, which is taken up from you into heaven, shall so come in like manner as ye have seen him go into heaven. Then return they unto Jerusalem from the mount called Olivet, which is from Jerusalem a sabbath day's journey." Acts 1:10-12 (See Matt. 24:30; 26:64 Mark 14:61-62; Acts 3:19-21; Rev. 1:7).

61. **Messiah will appear and Israel will be born spiritually "in one day":**

OLD COVENANT

"Who hath heard such a thing? Who hath seen such things? shall the earth be made to bring forth in one day? Or shall a nation be born at once? For as soon as Zion travailed, she brought forth her children." Isa. 66:8. "For behold the stone that I have laid before Joshua: upon one stone shall be seven eyes: behold, I will engrave the graving thereof saith the Lord of hosts, and I will remove the iniquity of the land in one day." Zech. 3:9 (See Isa. 10:17).

NEW COVENANT

"For I would not, brethren, that ye should be ignorant of this mystery, lest ye should be wise in your own conceits; that blindness in part is happened to Israel, until the fullness of the Gentiles be come in. And so all Israel shall be saved: as it is written, There shall come out of Zion the Deliverer, and shall turn away ungodliness from Jacob: For this is my covenant unto them, when I shall take away their sins." Rom. 11:25-27.

62. **Messiah will destroy all nations gathered against Jerusalem:**

OLD COVENANT

"For I will gather all nations against Jerusalem to battle; and the city shall be taken, and the houses rifled, and the women rifled, and the women ravished, and half of the city shall go forth into captivity, and the residue of the people shall not be cut off from the city. Then shall the Lord go forth, and fight against those nations, as when he fought in the day of battle." Zech. 14:2-3 (See Zech. 12:3-4).

NEW COVENANT

"And I saw heaven opened, and behold a white horse; and he that sat upon him was called Faithful and True, and in righteousness he doth judge and make war . . . And out of his mouth goeth a sharp sword, that with it he should smite the nations: and he shall rule them with a rod of iron: and he treadeth the winepress of the fierceness and wrath of Almighty God. And he hath on his vesture and on his thigh a name written, KING OF KINGS, AND LORD OF LORDS." Rev. 19:11, 15-16.

63. **Messiah will introduce the Millennial reign:**

OLD COVENANT

"And his feet shall stand in that day upon the mount of Olives, which is before Jerusalem on the east . . . And the Lord shall be king over all the earth: in that day shall there be one Lord, and his name one." Zech. 14:4a, 9 (See Isa. 11:1-10; 35:1-10).

NEW COVENANT

"And he laid hold on the dragon, that old serpent, which is the Devil, and Satan, and bound him a thousand years . . . Blessed and holy is he that hath part in the first resurrection: on such the second death hath no power, but they shall be priests of God and of Christ, and shall reign with him a thousand years." Rev. 20:2, 6.

64. **Messiah will rule over all nations:**

OLD COVENANT

"And it shall come to pass, that every one that is left of all the nations which came against Jerusalem shall even go up from year to year to worship the King, the Lord of hosts, and to keep the feast of tabernacles." Zech 14:16 (See Isa. 66:23; Psa. 45:6-7).

NEW COVENANT

"And out of his mouth goeth a sharp sword, that with it he should smite the nations; and he shall rule them with a rod of iron: and he treadeth the winepress of the fierceness and wrath of Almighty God. And he hath on his vesture and on his thigh a name written, KING OF KINGS, AND LORD OF LORDS." Rev. 19:15-15 (See John 5:28-29; Rev. 19:11).

65. **Messiah will bring world peace:**

OLD COVENANT

"And he shall judge among the nations, and shall rebuke many people: and they shall beat their swords into plowshares, and their spears into pruninghooks: nations shall not lift up sword against nation, neither shall they learn war any more." Isa. 2:4.

NEW COVENANT

"But every man in his own order: Christ the first fruits; afterward they are Christ's at his coming. Then cometh the end, when he shall have delivered up the kingdom to God, even the Father; when he shall have put down all rule and all authority and power. For he must reign till he hath put all enemies under his feet." 1 Cor. 15:23-25.

66. **Messiah will have dominion for ever and ever:**

OLD COVENANT

"For unto us a child is born, unto us a son is given: and the government shall be upon his shoulder: and his name shall be called Wonderful, Councillor, The Mighty God, The Everlasting Father, The Prince of Peace. Of the increase of his government and peace there shall be no end, upon the throne of David, and upon his kingdom, to order it, and to establish it with judgment and with justice from henceforth even for ever. The zeal of the Lord of hosts will perform this. Isa. 9:6-7 (See Psa. 72:8; Dan. 7:14).

NEW COVENANT

"And from Jesus Christ, who is the faithful witness, and the first begotten of the dead, and the prince of the kings of the earth. Unto him that loved us, and washed us from our sins in his own blood, And hath made us kings and priests unto God and his Father; to him be glory and dominion for ever and ever. Amen." Rev. 1:5-6 (See Phil. 2:9-11; Luke 1:32-33).

67. **Messiah is the Prophet:**

OLD COVENANT

" I will raise them up a Prophet from among their brethren, like unto thee, and will put my words in his mouth; and he shall speak unto them all that I shall command him. And it shall come to pass, that whosoever will not hearken unto my words which he shall speak in my name, I will require it of him." Deut. 18:18-19.

NEW COVENANT

"Then those men, when they had seen the miracle that Jesus did, said, This is of a truth that prophet that should come into the world." John 6:14. "For Moses truly said unto the fathers, A prophet shall the Lord your God raise up unto you of your brethren, like unto me; him shall ye hear in all things whatsoever he shall say unto you." Acts 3:22 (See John 1:45).

68. **Messiah is the Priest:**

OLD COVENANT

"The Lord hath sworn, and will not repent, Thou art a priest of for ever after the order of Melchizedek." Psa 110:4.

NEW COVENANT

"And no man taketh this honour himself, but he that is called of God as was Aaron. So also Christ glorified not himself to be made a high priest; but he that said unto him. Thou art my Son, today have I begotten thee. As he saith also in another place. Thou art a priest for ever after the order of Melchizedek." Heb. 5:4-6 (See Heb. 2:17-18; 6:20; 7:15-17).

69. **Messiah is the King:**

OLD COVENANT

"Rejoice greatly, O daughter of Zion, shout, O daughter of Jerusalem: behold, thy King cometh unto thee: he is just, and having salvation; lowly, and riding upon an ass, and upon a colt the foal of an ass." Zech. 9:9 (See Zech. 14:16). "Behold, the days come, saith the Lord, that I will raise unto David a righteous Branch, and a King shall reign and prosper, and shall execute judgment and justice in the earth. In his days Judah shall be saved, and Israel shall dwell safely; and this is his name whereby he shall be called, THE LORD OUR RIGHTEOUSNESS." Jer. 23:5-6.

NEW COVENANT

"And Jesus, when he had found a young ass, sat thereon: as it is written, Fear not, daughter of Zion: behold, thy King cometh, sitting on an ass's colt." John 12:14-15. "And it was the third hour, and they crucified him. And the superscription of his accusation was written over, THE KING OF THE JEWS." Mark 15:25-26 (See Matt. 27:11; Luke 1:30-35; John 18:36-37).

70. **Messiah, our shepherd, is God with all power:**

OLD COVENANT

"I saw in the night visions, and, behold, one like the Son of man came with the clouds of heaven, and came to the Ancient of days, and they brought him near before him. And there was given him dominion, and glory, and a kingdom, that all people, nations, and languages, should serve him: his dominion is an everlasting dominion, which shall not pass away, and his kingdom that which shall not be destroyed." Dan. 7:13-14 (See Psa. 8:6 and Heb. 2:6-10). "Give ear, O Shepherd of Israel, thou that leadest Joseph like a flock; thou that dwellest between the Cherubim, shine forth." Psa. 80:1. "Therefore the Lord Himself shall give you a sign; Behold, a virgin shall conceive, and bear a son, and shall call his name IMMANUEL. (God with us)." Isa. 7:14. "For unto us a child is born, unto us a son is given: and the government shall be upon his shoulder: and his name shall be called Wonderful, Councillor, The Mighty God, The Everlasting Father, The Prince of Peace." Isa. 9:6

NEW COVENANT

"For he must reign, till he hath put all enemies under his feet. The last enemy that shall be destroyed is death. For he hath put all things under his feet. But when he saith all things are put under him, it is manifest that he is excepted, which did put all things under him. And when all things shall be subdued unto him, then shall the Son also himself be subject unto him that put all things under him, that God may be all in all." 1 Cor. 15:25-28 (See Rev. 19:11-16). "I am the good shepherd: the good shepherd giveth his life for the sheep." John 10:11. "And she shall bring forth a son, and thou shalt call his name JESUS: for he shall save his people from their sins. Now all this was done, that it might be fulfilled which was spoken of the Lord by the prophet, saying, Behold a virgin shall be with child, and shall bring forth a son, and they shall call his name IMMANUEL, which being interpreted is, God with us." Matt. 1:2223. "Philip saith unto him, Lord, show us the Father, and it sufficeth us. Jesus said unto him. Have I been so long time with you, and yet has thou not known me, Philip? he that hath seen me hath seen the Father; and how sayest thou then, Show us the Father?" John 14:8-9. "And without controversy great is the mystery of godliness; God was manifest in the flesh, justified in the Spirit, seen of angels, preached unto the Gentiles, believed on in the world, received up into glory." 1 Tim. 3:16.

TESTIMONIES GIVEN SOME 2 000 YEARS AGO ABOUT THE MESSIAH

1. (Lord): "I will declare the decree: the Lord hath said unto me, thou art my Son; this day have I begotten thee." Psa 2:7. 2. (God): "This is my beloved Son, in whom I am well pleased; hear ye him." Matt. 17:5b. 3. (Jesus): "For had ye believed Moses, ye would have believed me: for he wrote of me."

John 5:46. “The woman saith unto him, I know that Messiah cometh, which is called Christ: when he is come, he will tell us all things. Jesus saith unto her, I that speak unto thee am he.” John 4:25-26.